RELAXATION
in a week

Pat and Colin Dyke

D1390874

Headway · Hodder & Stoughton

ACKNOWLEDGEMENTS

Every effort has been made to obtain permission to use quoted material in this book. The authors and publisher are grateful to the following for supplying photographs:
Mike Daniels Photography : Cover and pages 5, 6, 8, 11, 12, 15, 17, 19, 20, 22, 25, 28, 29, 31, 36, 39, 41, 44, 45, 37, 54, 59, 61, 64, 65, 68, 71, 73, 74, 77, 81, 83, 85, 86, 88, 99, 91, 94, 95, 99, 101, 102, 104, 106 and 107.
Richard Dyke Photographs: Pages 23, 55, 75, 79, 92 and 97.
J. Allan Cash Photography: Page 34.

British Library Cataloguing in Publication Data
Dyke, Pat
  Relaxation in a Week. – (In a Week Series)
  I. Title   II. Dyke, Colin   III. Series
  613.7

ISBN 0 340 56152 1

First published 1992

Typeset by Rowland Phototypesetting Ltd, Bury St Edmunds, Suffolk. Printed in Hong Kong for the educational publishing division of Hodder and Stoughton Ltd, Mill Road, Dunton Green, Sevenoaks, Kent by Colorcraft Limited.

CONTENTS

INTRODUCTION

Welcome to *Relaxation in a Week*. You have already made the decision to alter your lifestyle by reading this book. Many of us have lost sight of the senses that allow us to see, hear, touch, taste, feel and smell. These senses can be revived to enable us to make changes in our lives. We can renew the feeling of smelling flowers, touching petals, seeing the sunset, hearing music, tasting food we enjoy, and feeling happy. These sensations enable our minds to receive pleasure, comfort and joy. The ideas we present to you for relaxation and the exercises we offer you to reclaim the power of your senses have been devised through evening classes and workshops on stress management.

We all know that other people will want to advise us how to deal with our lives. This book will allow you to become your own therapist and friend. You may feel guilty spending time reading this book and allocating 20 minutes a day to do the exercises, but in life we often ignore our own internal message 'What about me?', so take note of your own needs and **do it**. After reading this book thoroughly and completely, not only will you benefit but those around you will gain from the new relaxed you. This book will help you understand that you can ask questions of yourself and make new choices. You have the ability to be more positive, contented, relaxed, calm and peaceful.

In nature all animals and plants need nurturing, stimulation, rest, relaxation and good growing conditions. As human beings we are also part of nature and, understanding that we have wonderful powers of adaptability, we need to train ourselves to create a normal, natural lifestyle.

INTRODUCTION

As you read this book you will learn to use the exercises which are included, and this will help you to deprogramme yourself to help you get rid of the stresses of modern civilised life. As the book develops we will focus on and explore the importance of breathing. We will move on to talk about using our minds to create images, words or feelings which can enhance and enable you to use imagery to refresh, renew and relax yourself.

We will give you the opportunity of exploring, both mentally and physically, different methods of putting yourself at ease. If you are going to change your lifestyle we will give you various ideas of how you can achieve this. It does require taking risks and trying out new experiences.

Stress is an essential ingredient of life and not enough stress can be as destructive as too much, for instance bored adolescents can wreak havoc. However, the relaxation techniques outlined in this book will give you numerous ways to counteract stress. During this week you will be taking the opportunity of re-evaluating your lifestyle, and as a result of this you will be able to give yourself more purpose, motivation and the desire to allow life to be fun.

This book will give you a sound basis on which to evaluate your life so far. It will give you many choices of how to view your approach to life from many different angles. It will enable you to look at interesting alternatives to help you to create a mind with whom you are on good terms. You may enjoy starting your day with mind and body working together to give you more energy and hope. Each day will become a new opportunity to find new skills and revive old ones.

At the end of the book we give a complete list of the exercises and visualisations we offer showing you how much time you need to allocate to each one. You can then select your own programme with the amount of time you have free. Take risks, try a new experience and vary the programme every day.

MONDAY

WELCOME TO MONDAY

I am only one, but I am one
I cannot do everything, but I can do something
And I will not let what I cannot do
Interfere with what I can do

This is the theme of the book. Remember you are unique, there will
never be another you. Read the poem again until you feel comfortable
with it. Allow your mind to review each line, and consider the
implications of what the poem tells you. You may wish to copy this poem
and put it where you can interpret its message every day.

In this chapter we focus on:
- The benefits of breathing correctly
- How to listen to and enjoy a tape
- Visualisation for Spring
- Exercise for self awareness

MONDAY

Breathing a new approach

Initially, we would like you to focus on your breathing. This is one of the automatic things we do in life. What is the purpose of breathing? How are you breathing now? As you are reading this paragraph breathe slowly three times in and out and notice how that feels. Most people are only aware of their breathing when something obstructs their nose and they cannot breathe freely and easily. We overlook the fact that when we breathe with more composure and control we allow more oxygen to reach and stimulate the brain.

Say to yourself, the slower I breathe the more energy I save, and the more easily I am able to absorb this book.

Spend time watching a cat or dog sleeping or relaxing and notice the way in which they breathe. When they inhale the rib cage expands and the stomach moves out as the air is drawn in. As they breathe out the rib cage and the abdomen contract, then there is a slight pause. This is the art of breathing in a relaxed manner.

If a plant is denied oxygen, as well as nutrients, sunlight and water it will not flourish. As we cherish a favourite plant so we should tend to our mind and body.

Relaxing positions for breathing

As it is your first day we will focus on a simple breathing exercise. As breathing is essential to your quality of life we will include other breathing exercises every day, so you may use whichever technique has meaning for you. As with many things in life, the more you put in the more knowledge you gain, so choose to do these exercises frequently. It is important for you to choose whether you want to sit or lie down. As time goes by and you try both, you will get to know more about yourself and your ability to relax in whatever position suits you. If you are sitting then make yourself as comfortable as you can. How are your legs? Where would you like to rest your hands? Do you enjoy having a cushion behind your back? Should you wish to lie down, do you lie on the settee, the bed or the floor? Do you require a pillow, or covers over you? Remember these are choices that you can make and by doing so increase the effectiveness of the exercise. Are you likely to be disturbed? Plan this time to give yourself the greatest benefits. There are a number of ways you can eliminate the possibility of being disturbed, including putting a **do not disturb** sign on your door.

Noticing your breathing pattern

Allowing yourself to keep your eyes open or closed we want you to notice your own breathing pattern now. Are you breathing from your shoulders? As you may know, when we are stressed and tense then we forget about breathing from the stomach. What speed are you breathing, is it fast or slow? Having noticed these feelings and how your body is reacting concentrate on making positive changes in your breathing which in turn will reduce any tension in your body.

Basic breathing exercise

- Is the air warm or cold?
- Is it flowing freely?
- Is your mouth open or closed?
- Take a deep breath and consciously slow the whole process down. Notice when you breathe in whether your stomach rises or falls.
- Now breathe out slowly and notice the physical changes that occur in your body.
- Breathe in again and become aware of the air passing in through your nose and see whether you can follow that air as it goes down into your lungs.

For many people breathing in through their mouth has become a habit. Is this happening to you? Keep your teeth slightly apart so your jaw is relaxed. Remind yourself that breathing in through the nose is more effective and is refreshing to both mind and body.

Now as you take a deep breath again say one to four internally and slowly. As you breathe out count from one to four again. Do this five times over. How is this for you? To give yourself a choice do the same exercise breathing from one to six. Is this more comfortable for you? Try it five times and then notice how you are sitting or lying. Is there any change? You may notice your hands getting warmer and starting to tingle. Repeat the exercise for three minutes using whichever sequence is most suitable for you. Enjoy the pleasure as you begin to achieve a healthier approach to your breathing, recognising that the more oxygen the brain receives the more effectively it can function.

You may have found during this exercise that your concentration was wandering. Understand that this is a natural reaction when you are in training for a new way of life. The more you practise the better your mind will focus.

Relaxation by tape

In this book there are a number of exercises and visualisations which ask you to carry out a sequence of instructions. You may find it beneficial to make your own tape. We set out guidelines in the appendix as to how you can do this successfully so you can enjoy your recording and benefit from the various exercises. If you prefer the sound of someone else's voice, ask a relative or friend to record this for you. You may have fun doing it together.

Enjoying your tape

In our busy lives when we try and do something to benefit ourselves it may be put to one side as a waste of time. If you can manage to arrange time to listen to your tape once or twice a day then you will be more relaxed and better able to organise, plan and carry out tasks in a way more acceptable to yourself.

Preparing to listen to the tape

We would suggest that you prepare yourself for listening to the tape by creating sufficient time to slow down before you switch it on. You can take some deep breaths in preparation and slow down the task you are performing. Tell those around you that you require 20 minutes to yourself, that you intend doing this by going upstairs to a bedroom, sitting in a car or even a bathroom. The tape should never be played when the car is in motion. Put a **do not disturb** sign on the door and make sure you keep the tape in an easily available place close to where you will listen to it.

Many of our clients find a Walkman or headphones attached to a stereo the best way to listen, but experiment and see what is right for you. Listen to the tape playing softly, this increases your concentration and subsequent level of relaxation.

MONDAY

Should your mind wander gently bring your attention back to the soft voice of the tape remembering the more you practise the easier it becomes, the easier it becomes the better you feel, the better you feel the more you are able to cope with life. You are renewing physical and emotional batteries, adjusting your heart rate, lowering your blood pressure, calming your digestive system and breathing patterns. This is good preventative stress proofing allowing you to become your own therapist able to control your mind and body.

Response to tape

The following may occur when you are listening to the tape:

- Eyelids flicker
- Arms get heavier
- Arms get lighter
- Hands get warmer
- Hands tingle
- Whole body feels heavy
- Whole body feels warm

All these sensations are natural and pleasant and need not concern you. You may experience different sensations. Everyone is unique and there is no right way or wrong way for anyone. Trust your mind and body and focus on the sensations you are feeling and tell yourself you are letting go. This is the time for renewal, peace and comfort.

Should you fall asleep while the tape is playing the words will still reach your subconscious mind. When the tape finishes either sleep, if this is appropriate, or return to full awareness feeling refreshed and fully in control.

You may find it useful to play the tape at night as an aid to going to sleep. Many of our clients also use a tape if they wake up during the night. They find this helps them regain a state of peace and tranquillity.

If you are able to use the tape on a regular basis this is preferable to listening only when you are stressed and anxious. Each time you will notice that your mind and body respond more easily and naturally, helping you to form new and good habits to keep you healthy and stress free.

Visualisation

Another interesting and important part of your new way of life will be **visualisation**. This is a technique using the creative part of your mind in a positive way. With practice your mind will be able to develop pictures from the various descriptions we offer in this book. Your mind is willing and able to adapt the images we offer into whatever is right for you. For some of us these images may not be as clear as we would like, but given time and practice the technique will become more effective. With these images you will find that the rewards are not only visual, you may also experience feelings of calmness and relaxation. In addition, your mind may also introduce sounds and smells to enhance the pictures.

As we point out in this book, nature is free so why not take advantage of it both in your mind and also in reality. There may be a particular experience in your life where you have been into the countryside and felt a profound sense of peace and tranquillity – why not recreate this in your mind in the next few minutes?

Your body can respond to visualisation just as if it were a real experience. This technique aids relaxation, healing and positive thinking. It also helps to maintain good health in mind and body. People are often health conscious and aware of the sort of food they are eating, but do not pay enough attention to the thoughts they are putting in their mind. The mind needs to be nourished as well as the body.

Preparing for visualisation

Read through the following visualisation carefully, then sit or lie comfortably and read the first lines again. Close your eyes, start breathing deeply and see, feel or hear the words you have just read.

Build up a positive picture you can focus on for a few minutes and then open your eyes and notice if your body feels more relaxed. Go through the visualisation in this way, piece by piece, and then open your eyes and check how involved you became. How does your body feel?

If you find it appropriate, when you have dealt with the visualisation in small sections, lengthen the sections until you are able to visualise the whole image.

Visualisation for Spring

Sitting comfortably, gently close your eyes and allow your mind to develop this country scene. Take as much time as you need to allow your mind to settle. Imagine yourself walking in the countryside on the first beautiful day in Spring. After a long dark winter it feels good to see the sun getting higher in the sky and you notice how warm it feels on your face.

As you walk down a narrow country lane with grass verges and low hedges winding down a hill you become aware of the country smells and sounds. At each bend in the lane a new vista opens up. Can you see wild flowers, grassy bank and fields with sheep grazing and lambs gambolling? You may choose to stop and listen to the sounds the sheep and lambs make and notice their contentment with and enjoyment of their surroundings.

As you reach the bottom of the lane, before it starts to wind up a hill, you notice a small stream gently meandering. The stream has steep banks and you may notice wild primroses. What else can you see, feel or hear? The air smells fresh and clean and you sit down and observe insects gliding over the water, a moorhen on her way downstream darting in and out of overhanging reeds. You may choose to follow the path of a twig as it floats along, eventually coming to rest against the bank. As you notice the reflection the sun creates on the water you feel at peace with yourself. Can you hear a church clock chiming in the distance? As you look up do you see fluffy white clouds drifting across the sky?

When you are ready, you make your way along the lane and follow a footpath up the hill that leads to a small coppice. The footpath is softer than the lane. How does this feel on your feet? You quicken your pace enjoying the energy your body provides to reach the top of the hill.

As you reach the coppice you hear the sound of a cuckoo in the distance, and as you listen you realise that birds of all shapes and sizes are

wheeling, dipping and darting in the sunshine. You hear the joyful sound they make and watch some of them settle in the trees.

You notice the trees have formed thick buds. If you touch these are they hard, or soft and sticky? In contrast you may notice the bark of the tree is firm and crumbly. Would you like to see how it feels to you?

As you are at the top of the hill you turn and enjoy the view of green fields and twisting lanes with the stream at the bottom. What colours can you see? You have a sense of oneness with nature and as you retrace your steps you enjoy the feeling of a breeze touching your hair, and more fluffy clouds racing across the sky. You are pleased that you went on your walk, and that you have the choice of repeating it on another day.

If you feel like opening your eyes at the end of this exercise then do so. However, you may prefer to go into some deep breathing, and open your eyes when you are ready.

Self awareness

Good health is an essential ingredient of your daily life. Throughout this book we will be offering you relaxation exercises which will contribute to your mental and physical wellbeing. You can monitor your own health by noticing when you are limiting opportunities to create time for relaxation and choose to allow yourself more freedom of choice. Do you recognise when there is tension in your body, especially around the shoulders and the back of the neck? If you look in the mirror do you see a pleasant happy reflection of yourself? Your face can indicate, both to you and other people, that you are not a relaxed and happy person. With this in mind we would like you to carry out the following exercise which focuses on your facial muscles.

This exercise needs to be done in private as you may pull some funny expressions. Tensing different sets of muscles in your face will have a significant effect, not only in your facial area, but also in other parts of the body. It may also mean that for the rest of your life your face will be smooth, calm and relaxed. What a wonderful feeling that will be! Your breathing will also become more even and enable you to feel more in control.

Facial muscles

Sitting comfortably, focus on your face and decide whether it is easier to close your eyes. As you breathe in we want you to screw up every muscle in your face, your forehead, eyes and jaw. As you breathe out allow these facial muscles to become smooth and comfortable.

Jaw muscles

With your eyes closed press your teeth together firmly and notice how this affects your jaw muscles. Let the jaw muscles relax and see if you notice any difference. Your jaw muscles are constantly in use so when you are resting allow them to relax completely.

MONDAY

Forehead muscles

Screw your forehead up and notice the tension. Let the muscles relax and feel the difference. Let go and smooth the forehead muscles and give your whole head area a pleasant feeling of relaxation.

Eye muscles

Screw your eyes up tightly and notice this causes tension around the eyes and possibly all over your face. Let your eye muscles slowly relax and notice the difference. With your eyes gently closed, look up and to the right and feel the pull of the eye muscles; centre and relax them. Look up and to the left and feel the pull of the eye muscles; centre the eyes and relax them. Continue by looking down to the right, centring, down to the left, centring and allowing the eyes to relax fully and completely.

Mouth muscles

Tighten up your lips and notice when tension occurs. Relax the lips and feel the difference. Push the tongue up to the roof of the mouth. Let it lie gently at the bottom of the mouth and allow it to relax.

You may notice that as you do this exercise you automatically go into deep breathing which indicates your mind and body are becoming more comfortable.

How does your jaw/forehead/eyes/mouth feel?

Were some parts of the exercise easier than others?

Do you need to repeat any part of the exercise?

How is your breathing now?

Write out in a personal achievement chart 'Today I have enjoyed relaxing my face.'

Conclusion for Monday

Throughout this chapter we have given a gentle introduction into a way of life which will give you the potential to develop your positive side. We have emphasised the importance of breathing slowly and developing self awareness. We have also explained the benefit of using a tape and experiencing visualisation, and introduced some simple exercises to relax your facial muscles. All of these techniques will help you to relax. Our main aim has been to suggest that you have *choice*. We hope that you have identified with much that has been written. As each day unfolds we will clearly set out different programmes for you to explore and enjoy.

WELCOME TO TUESDAY

This is the second 24 hours of your new approach to life. If you had entered for a marathon you would recognise the need for training to be built up over a period of time to be successful. Training and practice are also essential ingredients for allowing relaxation to become second nature to you. Given time you will be able to move into relaxation with a minimum of effort and thus improve the quality of your life.

In this chapter we would like to introduce you to:

- Internal processes
- Approach to tasks
- Breathing exercise with numbers
- Getting in touch with your senses
- Physical activities
- Hobbies
- Complementary therapies
- Visualisation for Summer

TUESDAY

Internal processes

If you are a car driver or a passenger you may have noticed if you don't change gear going up a hill there is a reaction from the engine. Have you analysed the process as to what causes you to change gear?

Is it the visual view of the hill?

Is it the sound of the engine labouring?

Is it the feel of the car juddering?

If you relate this to your own life do you take note of your internal senses when they are warning you that you are over-stretching yourself? As you continue to read this book you will be able to review what you are doing and take a different approach. As an individual do you see life as an uphill struggle? Do you rush at it and run out of energy half way up the hill? If you pace yourself and go up the hill in an appropriate way you would reach the top with a sense of achievement and energy in abundance to deal with other matters.

As you become more aware of your internal processes, the way in which your mind and body react to current external situations, then you are more able to adjust to and cope with them.

Sit quietly for a moment and notice your own internal processes:

Are you giving yourself the message 'I will not be able to get through all I have to do today'?

Is your mind going round and round?

How are you feeling inside?

Is your breathing slow or fast?

Are you sitting in a relaxed position?

Once you become aware of what is happening inside yourself you have the opportunity of taking control and becoming more positive. Choose to review quietly what you would like to achieve during the day. Be honest with yourself and make this a probability rather than a possibility.

Approach to tasks

We recognise there are times during the day when you will find yourself in situations in which you have to carry out mundane tasks. Choose the way you will tackle these tasks getting pleasure from the skills and qualities your mind and body possess. See the beginning and end of the tasks. If there are many that irritate you, give yourself five-minute treat times. Decide when these will be before you start the task. Use the time

to do some deep breathing, do a short visualisation, have a stretch, a hot drink or something energising to eat. At the end of the five minutes bring your attention gently back to the task in hand with renewed enthusiasm.

During your five-minute break you may choose to do the following exercise which has had favourable feedback from members of our relaxation classes who find it beneficial.

Breathing exercise with numbers

As you read in Monday's chapter, deep breathing can give you essential oxygen and renew and refresh your mind and body. Allow yourself to get a mental image of yourself quietly breathing deeply and benefiting from needed rest and relaxation.

TUESDAY

Close your eyes gently. Take a deep slow breath. Exhale slowly and completely, expelling the last breath of air from your lungs. As you inhale, picture the number one in your mind while focusing on your breath. Hold your breath for three seconds. Exhale, and as you breathe out mentally picture the number two. Inhale again picturing the number three and focusing on your breath. Hold your breath for three seconds. Exhale slowly and completely picturing the number four. Inhale focusing on five. Hold your breath for three seconds. Exhale focusing on six. Remember to picture the number and focus on the breath you are inhaling. Inhale picturing number seven. Hold your breath for three seconds, then exhale picturing the number eight. Repeat the sequence from one to eight. Open your eyes slowly. Consider how you feel after completing the exercise.

Were you able to concentrate on the numbers?

Was it easier to inhale or exhale, or were both the same?

Are you calm and rested?

Do you need to repeat the exercise?

Whatever the outcome be pleased with yourself for spending some time on your breathing. Do you feel better for giving some thought to your own personal space?

Getting in touch with your senses

The pace of life today can cause us to become distanced from our senses of touch, taste, smell, sight and sound. Choose to sit down quietly and

reflect on whether you are using your senses, as fully as you can, to enhance your way of life. Imagine a cat enjoying its food, rushing to its plate, attention fully focused on what it is eating and afterwards replete and satisfied, washing and grooming itself. See a wine taster carefully sniffing wine knowing that his nose is able to tell the difference between all the wines he smells and tastes. Smells can put you in touch with happy memories from the past for you to relive again. Visualise the fun of stroking and playing with a puppy or kitten. Imagine the sound of water, a calm sea, rain pattering down, a fast moving stream. Use your eyes to look around your day as if you were looking at a picture painted by a famous artist noticing every detail. Each day is unique, give it new meaning by enhancing and extending your perception of the world.

Touch

Touch is underestimated and you can experiment by touching various objects and seeing how you feel about them. There are many different textures – what feels best to you – a warm fluffy blanket, a piece of silk, the feel of a rose petal, the choice is endless.

Taste

It is important that you enjoy the taste of food, that you really savour each bite and allow the food to be chewed in different parts of your mouth to taste the full flavour. Do you plan what you are going to eat, when, where, how? Give yourself time to enjoy preparing the food, sit down and give your full attention to what you are eating. You may choose to use one of your five-minute breaks to give some thought as to what foods you want to eat. Food is a necessary and vital part of your life. Give consideration to the best way of fuelling your mind and body to give yourself ongoing energy and vitality. If your car ran out of petrol halfway to your destination you would be frustrated and annoyed. See yourself as making a journey through each day fuelling yourself with food so you are prepared for the pleasures and tribulations of the day. Food can contribute to your meeting each challenge with enthusiasm and hope.

Smell

Focusing on your sense of smell, have flowers, perfume, pot pourri or anything that you enjoy smelling near you. When you experience some negative feelings smell the fragrance and see if this helps to calm your thoughts.

Sight

Choose to use your eyes to give your mind exciting images to work with. Choose something small to look at, indoors or out, noticing its shape,

colour, texture. Allow yourself to focus on this object for one minute. If this is pleasurable focus on something else. You may find your visual images lead to thoughts. Where did this object come from? Would it look better in another place? Daydreaming is a visual art and your mind will work better for being offered a change of scenery.

Sound

Finally, how can you use sound? You can choose to distance the sounds that irritate you by making them quieter in your mind or by focusing on something else. If you are talking to an angry person see if you can change their voice in your mind so they are not intrusive to you. This may have an impact on the way you respond to them. You can choose to make your own voice more pleasant to listen to. You can listen to it on a tape and adjust the sound, so it is pleasing to you. You may find you get a better response from other people by slowing your voice down, pitching it lower. Have fun experimenting. Finally, look forward to listening to pleasant sounds, the birds when you wake up in the morning, the kettle boiling for a first cup of tea, cooking and bubbling sounds, favourite music. How do your feet sound on the pavement? Are you walking upright and confident? Do your feet sound different if you are?

Can you focus on a favourite piece of music when your world becomes excessively noisy?

Your mind will be able to take advantage of your special offers to it. In stressful situations you are offering it many ways of problem solving. Using these methods you will feel calmer and able to deal with life at a less stressful level instead of life dealing with you.

Exercise for accessing senses and memories

Imagine building a safe home inside yourself where you can access these senses.

TUESDAY

Using your five senses can be a way of recalling happy and positive experiences from the past when your senses played a more major part in your life. This can create a feeling of wellbeing which can be of great benefit – try it! How does it feel?

You may find it helpful to label the doors of your safe home with **touch, taste, smell, sight, sound**. You can then open the appropriate door and go into the room which offers the particular sense you want to contact at that time. Have some fun with the chart given below and ask your mind how it interprets pleasure for you.

Pleasure chart – getting to know your senses

What are your three favourite sounds?

Why?

What three images give you the most pleasure?

Why?

What three smells make you feel good?

Why?

What three foods taste best to you?

Why?

What are your favourite things to touch?

Why?

When you have completed this you may surprise yourself by your choices. Write them out in your favourite colour ink to remind yourself that they have special meaning for you.

Physical activity

Maybe you would like to build some physical activity or hobby into your programme even if you don't consider yourself to be sporty. Look carefully at the type of exercise on offer in your area and ask yourself what is the best possible choice for you. Gentle rhythmic exercises such as swimming, cycling and walking are excellent ways to release tension both in mind and body. If you want to take up an energetic sport go slowly and build up gradually. The most important aspect is that you are going to get pleasure and satisfaction out of your chosen exercise. Do not become a slave to exercise. You can spend a lot of money buying all the latest gear and decide you must go running or jogging every night and then after a short time realise this is not for you. Better to choose to start with a comfortable baggy track suit and a sense of adventure.

We list a few types of exercise and hobbies below which you might like to consider.

Cycling

This is a relatively cheap and enjoyable form of transport. You can either buy a first-class bike for yourself or look for a secondhand one until you are sure you are going to enjoy cycling. Be sure to buy a bicycle with gears to help you on the hills. You need to use your bicycle at least three times a week to gain some benefit from it. You can get fun out of your bicycle all year round.

Swimming

Swimming is one of the best forms of exercise you can take. Many public pools are open early in the morning so you could fit in a swim before you go to work. The same may apply in the evening when you can swim before your evening meal. Breathe freely and swim smoothly. You can exercise your legs by walking in the pool or holding on to the bar or jumping up and down. You can enjoy many different experiences in water. You are also able to share this activity with other people and see how they get pleasure from the water.

Tennis/Badminton/Squash

Games you play with other people can be fun or deadly serious depending on how you feel both about the people and the game. All these games use a great deal of physical energy and are a marvellous idea for people who have sedentary jobs – but take it easy and build up gradually if you are a beginner. They are also good for using up negative emotions such as anger and frustration. If you are able to join a club this is an excellent way of enjoying other people's company and feeling that you are using your body in a way that will keep it fit and healthy.

Walking

You can choose to walk and enjoy the pleasure of being outside. You are presented with new visual images all the time and walking briskly is fun. Your body automatically becomes erect and you stride freely and easily. You have a sense of wellbeing in mind and body. You feel alive and enjoy every step. When you have finished your walk you feel emotionally

recharged, mentally alert and ready to carry out your next task. Even if you are at work all day, you can take a walk at lunchtime or within your coffee break in order to give your body the opportunity to enjoy movement and co-ordination.

There are many other exercises that will be beneficial to you and in this chapter we have hopefully given you some ideas to choose from. There is of course the added advantage that when you are exercising you are away from distractions and demands on your time. When you return you will have a renewed sense of purpose and energy because you have been out, given yourself a change of scenery and done something just for you.

Remember, if you are in any doubt about your physical health, always check with your doctor before taking up exercise.

Hobbies

There are many different hobbies which offer pleasure and interest. We give you a sample and suggest you look in your local library or Adult Education Centre for further ideas.

Fishing

Fishing is a fascinating hobby which you can do on your own or with a club. You become part of the water world in a river, canal or pond where you can see the insects and small water creatures. You can also go sea water fishing either on-shore or off-shore in a boat. This is an all weather sport which requires great skill and dexterity. There are many books written on fishing which you can borrow from your local library.

Bird watching

The joy of bird watching is you can do it from your own kitchen window. Get yourself a bird table and see who comes to feed from it. Alternatively, you can go bird watching all day which will provide you with fresh air, peace and quiet and maybe some new varieties of birds you have never seen before.

We have house martins who nest every year in May outside our bedroom window. We enjoy the sounds they make and seeing them travelling through the air is breathtaking. They make wild swoops and darts all around the house and then disappear into a small hole in their nest. When the babies are born the whole nest seems to vibrate with sounds and movement.

Tropical fish

Have you thought of having a tropical fish tank? Many people get a great deal of pleasure out of an aquarium containing a variety of fish and underwater creatures. You can make them very attractive with plants, rocks and sands. If you spend a lot of time at home you may find this is a very rewarding hobby.

Gardening

A garden, or even a window box, can offer many hours of pleasure and creativity. Choosing seeds or plants, clearing the ground and composting it, seeing your ideas come to fruition and flowers and vegetables grow strong and colourful gives you a sense of purpose and direction in life.

Pets

Pets can be a rewarding experience for many of us. We can be lonely in relationships or alone because of circumstances. With a pet you can be young and playful no matter what your age is.

Careful consideration should be given to what kind of pet you want. Dogs have the reputation of being our best friend, but like any other pet they need you for security, food, play and love. With a dog you also have the opportunity and responsibility to take it for a walk no matter what the weather. This may improve your health and give you more purpose in life. Talk to your pet, and if it is a budgie or a parrot, maybe it will talk back.

Cats can offer another experience. They are fairly independent but enjoy sitting on your lap. Stroking a cat is both reassuring and comforting. Animals often sense when we are feeling low and give us comfort and attention.

Think about whether you need a pet in your life. They do take up extra time, but can also be very rewarding.

Reading

Finally, a good story can provide an opportunity to escape and indulge your imagination without even having to leave your armchair. Stepping into a different world of fantasy or non-fiction can be thought provoking, enjoyable and stimulating. Your book is there for you to escape into at any time – try it!

Complementary therapies

We would also like to suggest to you a choice of complementary therapies that may be appealing. Some are beneficial for various medical conditions, whereas others aid relaxation. It is possible to learn

more about several of them at night school, or by buying a book which deals with a particular therapy. Most bookshops nowadays offer a choice of books on alternative therapies.

Aromatherapy

Aromatherapy uses our sense of smell to produce a healing effect. Essential oils can be used to treat a wide range of disorders. They can be added to your bath, inhaled, or massaged into the skin. Many oils are now available in health shops so you can try aromatherapy at home, but be sure to find out how to use the oils – there are lots of good books on the subject – or better still, consult a qualified practitioner.

Acupuncture

Acupuncture stimulates the natural energy flow in the body by inserting needles at specific points on the surface of the skin. It works by harmonising the inner rhythms of biological, spiritual and mental functions. Acupuncture may be available under the National Health Service so check with your family doctor. It may bring relief from pain and a change in mood from depression to optimism.

Reflexology

Reflexology is a type of therapeutic massage which is carried out on the feet. It is based on the principle that the body is divided into zones which correspond with points or reflexes on the feet. The theory is that energy runs through these zones in channels all over the body and down to the feet. Blockages may occur in these channels causing ill health, and reflexology has the effect of unblocking the obstruction and restoring wellbeing. This is a very relaxing form of therapy.

Autogenic training

This is available in our chapter relating to Thursday. See page 58.

Yoga

Yoga teaches relaxation, breath control, physical and mental exercise. It is a safe, gentle, non-competitive activity which helps you to stretch your body and exercise every part of it, improving your posture and suppleness. Your local Adult Education Centre may run classes where a qualified instructor will help you.

T'ai Chi

T'ai Chi is a Chinese martial art which is practised by performing smoothly flowing movements in a sequence. It exercises every part of the body and the basic movements are carried out in a slow calm manner. T'ai Chi can be practised by people of any age or physical ability, including children. It is intended to create a balanced harmony at a physical, emotional and spiritual level. It can teach you how to expend your energy in a controlled way.

Dance therapy

Dance therapy exercises the body, releases inner tensions and improves posture and muscle control. It can either be used in a relaxing manner or in a forceful way to use up negative emotions.

Auto hypnosis

This is available in our chapter relating to Wednesday. See page 37.

Meditation

Meditation is a mental exercise that will help you to achieve a relaxed state of mind. You should relax your body and take deep breaths noticing the breath entering and leaving your lungs. You need to sit comfortably concentrating on an object that you like. You can also choose a peaceful word to focus on and allow this word to fill your mind. For some people meditation is a way of life that enables them to remain calm and tranquil during their day.

There are many other complementary therapies that may help you. Look in the health section of your local bookshop or library.

Visualisation for summer

Sitting comfortably gently close your eyes and allow your mind to develop this scene. This is a new experience so give yourself time to absorb what is happening.

Imagine that you are standing at the top of a wide sandy beach. It is a perfect summer's day. You look around at the large sweep of the bay. What can you see? What can you hear? What can you feel? Are there any other people on the beach? The tide is out and you may be able to see the pale golden sand stretching into the distance. Small friendly waves are gently breaking on the shore. Seabirds soar over the beach, sometimes landing on the water and you marvel at the beauty of their flight.

The sun is shining and you feel the warmth of its rays on your skin. There is a soft breeze blowing which caresses the hair on your forehead. You notice the warmth of the sun tempered by the soft stirring breeze. What are you wearing?

You may decide to find a comfortable place to sit, and when you are ready you breathe in deeply noticing the delightful fresh smell of the sea. You may choose to spend some time with your eyes closed listening to the sound of the sea, breathing in the pure air and feeling the warmth and pleasantness of the day. As the sun gets higher in the sky you decide to walk to the edge of the water. As you stand up you notice the sand is soft and dry under your feet and you wriggle your feet in the sand. As you get nearer to the sea the sand changes in texture and becomes damper and firmer. Which sand do you prefer to feel?

There are small pools which you may wish to step into. They are shallow and warm and it is fun to splash your feet in them. The sound of the small waves attracts you and you may notice how the sound changes as the waves come in and as they go out. You anticipate how you will feel when the sea runs over your feet. Will it be cold or warm? You stand at the water's edge listening to the sound of the sea and watching the water sparkle in the sun. Your mind is totally absorbed in all the sensations you are receiving. You may choose to spend time taking some more deep breaths as you enjoy the feeling of the water running over your feet. As the next small wave comes in you move slightly forward and feel the rush of the water around your feet and ankles. It feels exhilaratingly cold in contrast to the warmth of the sun, and your mind and body feel tranquil and calm as you allow them to be part of nature enjoying this perfect day. You can choose to go for a walk along the water's edge, noticing everything you see, hear or feel or you may turn and walk back up the beach, noticing the warm sun is now on your back. You see the welcoming sight of your towel, clothes, maybe a book, a cool drink and food to eat. You may choose to sit down, feeling relaxed and at ease, knowing you have choices about how you will spend the rest of your day.

When you are ready, let this picture slowly fade from your mind. At this time you may choose to do some deep breathing again, noticing that you feel relaxed and peaceful. When you slowly open your eyes you bring back with you all the good feelings that you have experienced. You are then able to continue your day with a calm and healthy mind and body, knowing that you can create this scene whenever you want to.

Conclusion for Tuesday

Today we hope that you have discovered that by taking note of your internal processes and the senses with which you perceive the world, you can change and improve the way you deal with everyday events in your life. You can also improve your life by taking up a new interest – a sport or hobby – to broaden your horizons or trying a complementary therapy to enhance your physical wellbeing. Thinking about and choosing new ways of living are important elements of your relaxation programme.

WEDNESDAY

WELCOME TO WEDNESDAY

Now you have arrived at Wednesday. We hope you are enjoying the book and are able to look at your week in a positive and buoyant way. In this chapter we will concentrate on hypnosis techniques and advise on sleep.

We discuss and offer the following topics:

- Handy hints for effective relaxation
- Self hypnosis exercises
- Conscious versus subconscious
- Visualisation for Autumn
- Bedtime sequence
- Positive sleep thoughts

Handy hints for effective relaxation

We recognise that several of the techniques we present take time to complete so we have set out some simple handy hints which we hope will be of value.

WEDNESDAY

Have a special chair for when you are feeling good.

Have a particular chair to sit in when you are worried and only use it for this purpose.

Notice something you like when you wake up in the morning, a picture on the wall or a photograph, and position it so it is the first thing you see.

Be unique but also be part of the universe.

If you live with someone else worry about their problems and let them worry about yours.

Smile at people, even if they don't smile at you this time. They may smile next time you meet or stop.

Store good memories. We watched a wonderful programme about the monsoon in India recently. Indians love their life giving rain. Maybe we could see our grey days as special.

Live today not yesterday or tomorrow, yesterday has gone and tomorrow has yet to come.

Look at the person you are inside and keep an image of that person.

Every moment is a new creation.

The outside person who is fat, thin, old, bald, young, spotty need not affect you the inside person.

Live your life in the fast lane and you will burn yourself out. Live your life in the slow lane and you will be bored. Live your life in the middle lane and you will reap tremendous rewards.

Plan a perfect day, week, year, life.

When you have unwanted thoughts put a large red stop sign in your mind.

Self hypnosis

All hypnosis is self hypnosis and we are now going to help you to learn these skills. As you will discover with practice these techniques can take as little as 10 seconds or as long as you like. When your mind is quiet and tranquil it will accept positive suggestions and give your life a new purpose. When we are emotionally drained we are unable to lift our spirits and get our lives back on course. By creating time for self hypnosis we can recharge our batteries and have a more optimistic view of the present and the future.

If possible you should practise twice a day when your mind and body can step off the world and regain the feeling of peace and relaxation. While you are in this state of mind you are not unconscious or asleep but fully aware of what is going on around you. Should the telephone or the front door bell ring, you will have a choice of whether you respond to those sounds. The depth of self hypnosis will vary from time to time. As you become experienced with these exercises, you will be able to achieve your own natural depth which will enable you to become more refreshed. The deepening process can cause heaviness or lightness in your limbs. They may also feel pleasantly warm or tingly. As you go deeper into this state of mind you may experience a wonderful sinking feeling. If your head wants to fall forward or to either side this is another indication that you are achieving a deeper state of self hypnosis.

We are all unique and you may experience all, some or none of these different feelings. Do not worry if they do not all happen for you.

Self hypnosis – exercise 1

Sitting or lying in a comfortable position we would like you to concentrate on a point or an object in front of and slightly above you. As you concentrate on this point, become aware of your breathing. Notice that every time you breathe in your eyelids start to become heavier. You can reinforce this experience by saying in your mind 'My eyelids are getting heavier'. As you concentrate on the point or object you have chosen you become aware that your sight is becoming hazy. Continue this sequence until you reach a point where it would be easier to just close your eyes. You may become aware of a warm comfortable feeling inside. How is your breathing now? Have your arms become heavier or lighter? Does your body feel relaxed and comfortable?

Give yourself positive messages about what you want to achieve in your daily life.

When you are ready you can start to think about opening your eyes slowly, getting ready to return to the real world, allowing yourself a long stretch and enjoying a feeling of peace and calm.

Self hypnosis – exercise 2

Again sitting or lying comfortably, focus on a particular point or object and become aware of your breathing. Once you have focused on your breathing count from ten to one, associating the counting with breathing out. In your mind you can reinforce this process by saying 'Every time I breathe out and count down my eyelids will become heavier'.

10 Eyelids getting heavier and heavier.
 9 I am beginning to let go.
 8 My eyelids are getting heavier and feeling hazy.
 7 My breathing is even and calm. My breathing is even and calm.
 6 My eyes are getting hazier and hazier.

Continue counting down to one closing your eyes when you are ready.

To allow yourself to go deeper to your own natural level of self hypnosis, repeat the counting down sequence from ten to one remembering every time to count the appropriate number as you breathe out.

Take yourself in your mind to your favourite memory or fantasy which could be a beautiful garden, a walk in the woods, a beach or a mountain

range. Take as long as you want so you can bathe in the peace and tranquillity of this experience. While you are spending time with your mind and body at peace, reflect in a calm way on a particular difficulty or problem in your life. You may surprise yourself that in this state of mind you can take a different and more positive view of your situation. This may enable you to go forward in your life.

When you are ready to return to familiar surroundings, count from one to ten, breathing in on one, breathing out on two until you reach number 10. Open your eyes slowly and stretch, feeling more positive and optimistic about your life.

These exercises can be carried out at bedtime. They can be effective in helping your mind to be naturally relaxed so the quality of your sleep improves. We go on to talk about sleep and waking up exercises on page 45–52.

Self hypnosis spiral

You may like to try using the spiral illustrated below. So, sitting comfortably with the book resting on your lap, focus on your breathing, then concentrate on the spiral. As you do so your eyes will be drawn to the centre. As you focus on the centre your eyes may become hazy and it will be easy for you to close them. With your eyes closed, continue to breathe gently and evenly and remain in this relaxed state for as long as you wish. When you are ready to return to your daily life, slowly count from one to 10 telling yourself that when you open your eyes you will feel refreshed and revitalised.

WEDNESDAY

Blue bulb

Another alternative way of going into self hypnosis is by using a blue electric light bulb. After fitting your light bulb into a lamp sit down comfortably and concentrate on it. Breathe gently and as you do this you will find your eyelids become heavy and your eyelids hazy as you concentrate on the colour of the light. You may notice that the blue light separates, and within a short space of time you may find you want to close your eyes and go into self hypnosis enjoying the warm, comfortable feeling that is associated with this relaxation technique. Enjoy this experience for as long as you want, understanding that by counting from 10 to one, in association with breathing in and out, it will take you into a deeper relaxed state.

When you feel it is time to return to your daily life, count from one to five, opening your eyes on five, feeling pleased that you have taken this time to allow your mind and body to slow down.

Exercise for mind flexibility

Here is a scene you might choose to create during your self hypnosis exercises.

Remind yourself that for the next few minutes you can let go of any stress or tension. We want you to picture in your mind one of your favourite scenes and create this image in black and white, do not try too hard, as this may affect the clarity of your image. Just let the image come gently into your mind.

Take three more deep breaths, and gradually let the artistic part of your mind put colour into the image, and, if it is appropriate, introduce sounds and smells which are relevant to your image.

WEDNESDAY

Did you notice any change in how you felt as you introduced colour into your image? If you were not aware of any reaction you could maybe change the image back to black and white, and repeat the exercise. Stay with this experience for as long as you feel comfortable and then return to full awareness of everything around you.

With practice you will find that this technique can be effective in promoting a more healthy and positive approach to life. You may not be able to change the circumstances of your life, but you can change the way you respond to them.

Another benefit from this exercise is, if in the depths of winter the day is cloudy, even if there is snow and frost on the ground, you can sit looking out of your window and identify significant points of interest. Close your eyes and using the power of your mind, introduce a blue sky, trees with leaves, pretty flowers. Put all these things into your scene and observe how this can change your view of what is outside the window. You can, if you want to, picture how it looks outside in spring, how it looks outside in summer, how it looks outside in autumn, how it is looking right now. Your mind is adaptable and flexible and you can produce any image that you prefer. You may find it helpful to open your eyes every now and again just to check how the outside image compares with the one you are picturing. Close your eyes to enhance the effect and notice the difference between the outside image and your internal one.

Conscious versus subconscious

The conscious mind will reason and decide what course of action it wants to take, but it needs agreement from the subconscious. When an agreement is made the subconscious will direct its vast energy into fulfilling your desires. The subconscious works exactly like a computer and started recording and storing information before you were born.

Both parts of the mind need to work in harmony. In hypnosis, meditation and relaxation the conscious mind is quietened enabling the subconscious to listen to the messages we want it to hear. The subconscious in its amazing way records every sound, taste, touch, smell, feeling we have ever experienced. By accessing it we can recall long forgotten happy memories. By giving new and relevant information as to how we want it to act now, the subconscious will use its vast store of wisdom and energy to supply us with solutions more appropriate to our present needs.

The subconscious allows you to visualise and imagine in a positive or negative way. You can imagine you are going to pass your driving test, be successful in a business interview, make a delicious cake, be captain of a football team and your subconscious is happy to help you. You can also imagine nobody loves you, you are useless at games, you are the world's worst typist and the subconscious will help you to realise these messages in exactly the same way. These are the messages you are giving yourself and your subconscious will accept and reinforce this as being what you want.

The incredible energy of the subconscious is available to you in a positive way if you choose to spend some time quietening the conscious mind and working on a program for the subconscious which is suitable for your present day requirements. We hope you make this choice as it will be one of the most exciting and rewarding things you ever do. You cannot expect to program a computer with a faulty program and then expect correct results. Programming your own computer to work for you gives you the choice of editing out negative emotions, deeds and actions and editing in love, joy, pleasure both in work and play.

If you use your subconscious to see positive end results instead of tedious tasks your world can improve. Negative emotions such as fear, anger and frustration deplete the energy that our subconscious mind can offer us. These emotions require boundless energy which the subconscious is willing and able to generate. However, this leaves you without the energy to enable you to feel joy, pleasure, reward and fulfilment which are all there waiting for you to change channels. The press and the media are often responsible for giving us negative messages which can make us feel sad and angry. You can choose what food you put into your body. In the same way you can choose what images or messages you put into your mind. If you programme in some pleasant thoughts every day you are giving your mind positive feedback which enables you to look at your own life with direction and purpose.

Visualisation for Autumn

Go out of the house on a still and perfect golden morning in autumn. Take yourself into an orchard where the apple trees are ripe and weighed down with glorious apples in every shade of green and red. Maybe it can be your own orchard and you have carried large wicker baskets and a ladder to pick the fruit. On this still and peaceful day you feel ready and able to work on this task of gathering the fruit. You place your ladder against a tree and climb up into the branches, noticing how your feet and legs are strong and able to push you from rung to rung. All around you are leaves, branches and apples, and from the top of your ladder you can also see a tall castle with eight turrets in the distance. The castle has stood there for centuries and, for a moment, you imagine how life might have been at that time. In your mind, you float over the battlements and arrive in the courtyard and see a great jousting tournament where hundreds of people have arrived to see knights in shining armour thunder towards each other on sturdy horses. You can hear the sound of lances hitting each other and the roar of the crowd as the favourite knight jumps from his horse and bows in victory. Could this knight be you? All around are colourful scenes of food being prepared, meat roasting on a spit, vegetables bubbling away in the castle kitchens. You smell the richness of the food. Busy servants are hurrying about getting ready for the mammoth feast to be held in the castle when the jousting tournament is over. A wandering troupe of minstrels strolls through the crowd and all around you there is merriment and dancing.

Your mind returns to your ladder in the apple tree and you wonder if apples were grown around the castle at that time. You pluck an apple from the tree and feel its roundness and warmth in the sun, and you taste it and notice it is juicy, firm and crunchy. Hopefully you will collect enough apples to be able to store them through the cold winter months. Every time you eat one you can remind yourself of how you picked them on this lovely autumn day.

WEDNESDAY

Bedtime sequence

We hope that the final theme for Wednesday will help you to relax at the end of the day.

Do you take the cares and worries of the day to your bedroom or do you feel at ease the moment you open the door and go inside? Do you allow yourself time for a pleasant bath or wash? Are you able to remove your clothes slowly, shedding the cares of the day with them? Can you take pleasure in getting out clean clothes for the morning? Can you choose to get into a calming down routine and remind your body that it has the right to relax and renew itself for the day ahead? Can you explain to other people in your house the benefit of this slow routine so they understand why you have chosen to do it? Maybe they will be able to experience its value as well.

Can you choose to stay with this day and enjoy the end of it? Yesterday has gone and tomorrow has not yet come. Is it easier for you to go to bed earlier and get up earlier, transferring certain tasks to the morning when you are rested and refreshed? Can you allow night time to be a slowing down and easing up time? At stressful times during the day, can you picture yourself in your bedroom at night, comfortable and secure, perhaps with a book or soft music. This image can give you the strength and energy to carry out boring or routine tasks.

Changing statements

Make a list of good things about night time. It is quieter than daytime, dark and restful. What can you add to your list? The thoughts you have about sleep decide the quality of sleep you enjoy.

You may lie in bed thinking:

- I know I won't sleep.
- There are two cars next door that are very noisy and always arrive after midnight so what's the point in trying to sleep.
- I should have washed the floor, the dog, the cat, the baby, me.
- I hate going to work.

How about changing these statements around to more positive thoughts:

- I enjoy relaxing my mind and body and going to sleep.
- I am so relaxed when I am asleep that any noise I hear just allows me to go deeper and deeper. Should any sound need my attention then I will deal with it and return to my normal restful sleep which I deserve and need at the end of the day.
- I shall have boundless energy tomorrow and have listed the tasks which I feel are important for me to do.
- I take pride and pleasure in the work that I do though some aspects of it do not appeal to me.

Put the second list of statements by your bed and perhaps list some more. Remember when you get disturbed at night it is not the waking up that is a problem, it is the angry feelings about being disturbed that will keep you awake. Leave outside noises where they belong, outside your bedroom.

Positive sleep thoughts

Another pleasant thought is that even when you sleep you are able to adjust your body to a more comfortable position. You will know when to pull the covers up around your neck or throw them off if you are too warm. Choose to tell yourself that when you wake up you will be refreshed and looking forward to the day. Be prepared to give some time to this thought. If your mind has been receiving negative signals it may take a little time to adjust to positive ones – but it will happen!

Go through the pleasant sleep exercise we give in this chapter and give your muscles instructions that the day is for work and fun, the night is for relaxation and every muscle will become completely and wonderfully at ease and remain that way until you wake up in the morning. Learning to relax at night is an enormous bonus which will enable you to meet each day with good humour, pleasure, and a feeling of what exciting happenings may occur today.

WEDNESDAY

When you have mastered the fantastic art of relaxation then you may be able to give yourself instructions at night as to what dream you would like, or continue a dream from one night to the next. Close the door on your troubles at night and the possibilities are endless for you to open the door to a successful day in the morning.

Sleep tape

You may find that the easiest and most pleasant way to have a restful and comfortable night's sleep is to record the following exercise onto a tape, slowly and evenly, and play it to yourself when you have settled in your bed and your mind and body are looking forward to a wonderful sleep. Turn the light out, settle down, turn the tape on and listen to your own voice soothing you. Thank yourself for dealing with your day in the best possible manner and then get ready for your pleasant listening time.

Exercise for sleep

'Now that I am in bed I will get in my most comfortable position. I will listen to the tape and move around if I want to and that feels fine. If the tape continues after I have drifted off to sleep that is acceptable to me or if I listen to the end, that will also be pleasant and good for me. I will take a deep breath, as slowly as I am able. Every breath I take will help me to become more calm and relaxed. My mind may be wandering and focusing on events of today or concerns about tomorrow, but as I let go these thoughts will drift away and will be of little interest to me. I will breathe deeply from my tummy and notice how my head feels on the pillow. My eyes may be closed by now and my head is becoming heavier and heavier and I can feel it sinking into the pillow which is very pleasant. Are my shoulders comfortable? I will use the wonderful power of my mind to allow my shoulders to become heavier and heavier. I will go slowly through the rest of my body allowing each part of me to become heavier and heavier. Are my hands warm or cold? Am I experiencing a warm comfortable feeling inside? I can feel heaviness spreading through my body, my arms, down my legs to the tips of my toes. As I allow my body to become heavier and heavier I am aware of a pleasant feeling as I sink into the mattress and enjoy letting go.

'I may just screw up my eyes tightly, count to six and then totally release any remaining tension. I listen to my breathing and notice whether it is regular and even and I feel good about myself and my breathing. I tense my hands and arms to a count of six and then I let go. I take my attention into my fingers one at a time and allow each finger to rest comfortably. I tense my legs to a count of six and then let them go right down to the tips of every one of my toes. All the time my body is becoming heavier and heavier and I am now experiencing a beautiful warm feeling. My hands may feel warm and tingly and relaxation is taking place all through my mind and body.

WEDNESDAY

'The weight of my covers is just right for me and I am drifting and enjoying a hazy feeling in my mind as it becomes calm and settled. I will continue to allow myself to drift deeper and deeper. If I choose I will count from 10 to one, counting each number as I breathe out and I will tell myself I am going deeper and deeper. I enjoy these feelings of deep relaxation and if I need to I will go through all the parts of my body again. If there is the smallest area of tension I will simply let it go by breathing away. As I breathe out I will enjoy breathing away the discomfort and knowing I am in control, and I will allow myself to go deeper and deeper. I will continue to become heavier and heavier. If I choose to move into a more comfortable position this is fine. I will sink further and further into my mattress and enjoy going into profound relaxation.

Conclusion for Wednesday

As we are now in the middle of the week we felt this might be an appropriate time for you to focus on self hypnosis as a calming influence, and the benefits of natural sleep. You will appreciate that these techniques can have a powerful influence on giving you a more relaxing way of life. Why not try one of the exercises again? If your time is limited, select your own handy hints to help you through the day. As we have finished this chapter with relaxation techniques to help you sleep, we'll begin tomorrow with exercises to help you wake up gently and calmly.

THURSDAY

WELCOME TO THURSDAY

Here are the ingredients of today's chapter which we hope you
will enjoy:

- Wake up exercises for the body and mind
- Awareness of the outside world
- Pleasure selection
- Positive experiences
- Immediate visualisations
- Music for pleasure
- Effective listening
- Mental interpretation
- Internal awareness
- Autogenic training

Waking up exercises

Today, why not wake up and smile? This will relax your facial muscles
and then you can follow these simple exercises to compose yourself for
the day. You may find it helpful to complete an exercise to relax your
mind, or alternatively one to loosen up your body. Why not try them both
to see which suits you best?

Waking up exercises for the body

Part 1
When you have been asleep, it may be that your body is relaxed, so as
soon as you wake up, lie on your back looking up at the ceiling, and
place your hands behind your head allowing your elbows to rest in a
comfortable position. Bring your elbows towards each other, lift your
head and gently move it towards your chest. Hold for as long as this feels
comfortable. Return your elbows to a resting position. Repeat until you
become aware that your arms, shoulders and neck are feeling pleasantly
loose.

Still lying on your back with your covers rolled down and legs straight,
bend your right knee towards your body. Breathing out, clasp it loosely
with your hands and pull gently towards your chest. Try to let your waist
sink into the bed, extending your spine. Hold for a count of six. Release
your hands and gently place them by your sides and lower your leg
back to its resting position.

Repeat with your left leg. Well done!

Now, with both arms by your side in a relaxed position, bend both knees towards your chest. Raise your head gently towards your bent legs. Put both arms around your knees and hug yourself. Hold for a count of three. Lower your head gently, return your hands to your sides and allow your legs to return to their resting position.

Circle your ankles and hands in turn clockwise and then anti-clockwise.

Still lying flat with both arms over your head and keeping your elbows and knees loose, straighten your arms and legs and stretch your whole body from fingertips to tips of toes and hold for as long as it is comfortable.

Be pleased with the exercise you have now completed.

To help you get out of bed, roll on to your side and push yourself up sideways – especially if you have a bad back. Now sit on the edge of the bed and turn your head slowly towards your left shoulder and then towards your right shoulder. Stand up and gently shake your limbs to loosen them up. You can now choose to go on to Part 2 of the exercise, or you could try the exercise for waking up your mind.

Waking up exercise for the body

Part 2
Making certain that you are wearing sufficient clothing to keep warm, stand in front of a mirror and keeping your legs slightly apart, ensure that you are well balanced. Take 10 slow deep breaths, smiling as you do so. Then tense all the muscles of your face, body, arms, hands, legs and feet as you breathe in, seeing how you look in the mirror. Slowly release the tension as you breathe out, again checking how you look. Repeat this sequence three times.

Now push your shoulders up towards your ears trying to touch your ears and noticing any tension as you breathe in. Then let your shoulders drop into a comfortable position as you breathe out. How do you look? How do you feel?

Push your right shoulder up towards your right ear, doing the same breathing movement, and drop it. Then make the same movement with your left shoulder. Shake your arms and hands several times to release any tension.

As you breathe in, gently raise your right knee as far as you are able. Very slowly, as if in slow motion, let your leg return to the floor as you breathe out. Repeat the same with the left knee. Lift your right foot, get in touch with how it feels and shake it, releasing any tension. Do the same movement with the left foot. Return to your face and thank yourself with another smile for completing the exercise which has helped to prepare you for the busy day ahead.

Waking up exercise for the mind

Either sitting or lying, whichever is more comfortable, focus on a particular point on the ceiling or on an object, such as a vase of flowers, and concentrate on that point. Start to slow your breathing down as much as you can and tell your eyelids each time you breathe out that they are going to get heavier and heavier. Then start counting slowly from 10 to one, reinforcing that your eyelids are getting heavier and heavier and your vision is becoming pleasantly hazier and hazier. You can then give yourself permission to close your eyes. For the next two or three minutes create a mental picture of yourself going through your daily routine with a wonderful sense of inner calm. Affirm to yourself that you will use your day in a positive and satisfying manner. Run through the day in your mind gently and calmly and consider the options you have for dealing with different situations. This will enable you to foresee and anticipate certain difficulties that may arise so you can plan your time and energy in a constructive way. You can then count from one to 10 telling yourself you feel refreshed and ready to start your day. Open your eyes when you reach 10.

Awareness of the outside world

When you have completed the relaxation exercises, stretch every muscle in your body and then look with interest at your bedroom. Notice the objects that please you the most. Do you have pleasant pictures, pretty curtains, an attractive bedside lamp, soothing creams, fragrant perfumes or aftershave? What do you hear when you wake up in the morning? Are there birds outside? Can you think about the sounds that you like rather than the noises that you don't? Allow your foreground sounds to be the kettle boiling, the clatter of china being prepared for breakfast, the general pleasant bustle of the day ahead. Concentrate on how your body moves after the pleasant relaxation. You are able to have hopeful movements that release the energy for Thursday not tense, tight movements that tell your mind and body the whole day is going to be like climbing a mountain.

Pleasure selection

Choose to make a list of things that you really enjoy. Every day select a particular pleasure for yourself. We find in our classes people often select something that costs nothing like a bath, a walk, a favourite radio programme, which allows them to use their imagination. Choose to change your 'don't likes' into 'not so bads'. You have many undiscovered skills waiting to be used for your benefit. The doubts and fears can be placed in a file marked 'not for present use' and you can open up a new file marked 'joys and pleasures'. This file can be used for pleasurable times, such as eating, walking, music and many other experiences that are there for you to enjoy every day. You can still get out the 'doubts and fears' file, choose a particular problem and decide a future course of action for it. You may then be able to transfer it to the 'joys and pleasures' file as you will be able to take pleasure in your problem solving skills.

THURSDAY

Positive experiences

Sometimes at our classes people have rushed from work, are not able to park the car, have had to rush their meal or had no meal at all. These are all things which happen outside of themselves and which they are unable to control. However, they can control their reaction, they can breathe deeply, they can talk to their hands and ask them to feel heavier and warmer. They can see cloud formations, they can visualise, think of or feel happy memories, glorious sunsets. They can make lists either in their minds or in writing of how to plan their day. They can reward themselves during the day by allowing space for themselves. They can mentally win the tennis at Wimbledon, climb the highest mountain, cross a desert in a sandstorm.

Life is a tight rope along which you can walk with no thought of falling. Every age brings its own rewards and opportunity if you change internally. You have within you a confident, self assured, good humoured person and you have the ability to see, feel or think that you are in charge of your individual world. This day will be relaxing for you, your mind and body are willing and able to offer every encouragement, to choose to notice every good thing you see and store it for future pleasant reference.

Immediate visualisations

In this book we have suggested several long visualisations with considerable detail encouraging you to use your senses of touch, hearing, sight, taste and smell. We now suggest some ideas for short visualisations. Give each one your full consideration and see which appeals the most. Then, at a time that is appropriate to you, try the others. You may find your subconscious mind has different ideas to your conscious mind as to which one is best for you. Your mind may interpret these in pictures, words or feelings. Have fun trying them out.

A stream

Is your stream wide or narrow?
Does it wind or is it straight?
Where is it going?

A ride in a balloon

Where do you start from?
Where do you go?
Is it day or night time?
Is it comfortable in the basket?
What is the purpose of your journey?

A mountain

What is at the bottom?
Is there snow at the top?
Is it easy to climb?
Is there anyone with you?
Can you ski down it?

A house

How many rooms?
Old or new?
Who lives there?
Is this the ideal place for you?

An old children's book

What do the pictures show?
Who has read the book?
How does it begin?
How does it end?
What is the picture on the front page?

An erupting volcano

What noises does it make?
How does it smell?
Is it exciting or frightening?
What is the eruption like at the beginning?
At the end?
At the height of its eruption?
How does it make you feel?

An island

Cold or hot?
Windy or calm?
Mountainous or flat?
Do you live there or visit?
Does anyone live there?
Are they hostile or friendly?

An ideal person

Would this person be male or female?
How do they look?
How do they dress?
What do they do or say that is ideal?
What do they do with their lives?

A boat

Does it belong to you?
Does it sail or have an engine?
Is it big or small?
Does it go out to sea?
Would you spend a night on it?

A musical extravaganza

How big is the orchestra?
Is there a choir?
Indoors or outdoors?
Is there a soloist?
A conductor?
Are you watching, singing or playing?

THURSDAY

Was this exercise hard or easy? Where did you feel most at ease? Can the ideal person be you? This exercise enables you to go anywhere or see anything and it costs you nothing. It is good to do at any time but particularly if you are bored or alone.

You may find out some new things about yourself, which places are safe for you and which are not. See how you feel at the end and whether you want to retrace your steps and allow any of your images to be more tranquil and calm, or whether the excitement of a volcano or desert island enables you to get rid of hostile, aggressive feelings. Enjoy the experience.

Music for pleasure

We have just talked about a musical extravaganza. For most of us listening to music is satisfying and can create a feeling of wellbeing as we can link special memories to different songs or pieces. Singing, for many of us, is a way of expressing ourselves, but the place we choose to use our voice in a positive and rewarding way is usually the bathroom or the car, listening to a tape or radio programme. To sing as loud as you can, especially in a car where you are uninhibited, is both therapeutic and relaxing. Have you thought of writing down the lyrics to your favourite song? Have you thought of keeping them in a folder ready for use? You will then be in a position to sing whenever you want to.

Sometimes we listen to pieces of classical music, maybe we don't even know the title, but have a pleasant reaction when we hear the music played. Perhaps you have heard a piece on a television advertisement, which often use music written by well-known classical composers. Another way of enjoying music, even in a room where people are watching television, is to use a set of headphones. With little effort you can listen to your favourite piece of music and enjoy the finer points of the singer and the musicians. When you listen through the headphones and concentrate, you may be able to pick up the intricate backing and counter melodies which complement the instrument and the singer. Another alternative is to read a book with the music as a pleasant background sound.

Effective listening

A technique which we have developed, and has proved effective, is asking a person to sit in a room with a set of headphones on and concentrate on the way their mind, their ears and their feelings are reacting to the sound of silence. Somehow this allows an individual to tune in to their own internal experiences. This experience can allow the person to identify whether their mind at that point in time is hearing sounds, seeing pictures or linking up with feelings in any part of their body. This can have quite surprising results. The slight pressure created by the headphones can assist in focusing on how your mind is working.

Further effective listening

Another way of using headphones in a positive and productive manner, when you are surrounded by people occupied in activities that don't appeal to you, is to buy a tape of a book which you can then enjoy. This will probably be recorded by an actor or actress who is able to express the words in such a way that it may bring new meaning to the story. Many libraries have books on tape that you can hire cheaply. This is another way of escaping into a world of make believe and creating a feeling of relaxation for yourself. Remember story telling is older than the written word.

Radio listening

Have you thought of listening to the radio, either during the day, or in the evening? Take a look at the radio listings in the paper for today: There are all sorts of interesting programmes to listen to where you can create your own internal feelings. Sometimes this can be preferable to having them created for you by television and films.

Mental interpretation

The way you perceive life mentally, and how you approach or respond to things that happen can have an enormous effect on you. Are there voices in your mind? Are they pleasant or unpleasant, criticising or praising? Can you make them louder, softer, slower, more distant? Are you able to allow unpleasant words to become pleasant ones? Whose voice is speaking to you?

If you see pictures in your mind are they black and white, coloured, are they big, are they small, pleasant or unpleasant? Can you change the pictures quietly and firmly into ones that particularly appeal to you?

Do you choose to have unpleasant feelings? Can you find out what colour they are and choose a different colour and shape. Can you recognise unpleasant feelings and let them go? Take some deep breaths and reward yourself with a pleasant anticipatory feeling or a feeling from the past.

Use the power of your mind to change to whatever pictures, words and feelings are most rewarding and positive for you.

When you have finished this piece of work perhaps you would like to listen to a piece of music to relax yourself. See what internal changes you have made.

THURSDAY

Internal awareness

Ask your body to calm down on a regular basis and it will listen to you. Stress from outside sources is very real, but you can choose how you respond to it and you do not need to add to it by creating stress inside yourself. Keep the outside world where it belongs. Take the part of the world that you do enjoy inside yourself, and let the remainder keep its distance. You are a unique creation, and in order to maintain the perfect balance of mind and body you were born with, you need to choose to keep all outside influences in perspective. Enjoy what you can and deal with the rest by keeping your mind and body together.

Autogenic training

One of the safest and most pleasing ways of learning what your mind and body can do to allow itself to be relaxed, healthy and contented is autogenic training. Once you have acquired the fulfilling habit of breathing deeply then try this exercise. This is a well-known method of relaxation which you can use for a short period of time, concentrating on specific areas of your body. You can use it for just your arms and your legs. If you choose to allow more time for the relaxation of other parts of your body then this is fine. If you choose to take the opportunity of going forward in your life, in a relaxed way you are allowing your mind and body to move freely. Some people go through life as if they are struggling to move their arms and legs in water which is chest high. Walk on springy grass in your mind with your head held high and a smile on your face, and you will notice the difference in your daily problems. In order to give yourself the motivation to practise these exercises, look at yourself on a cinema screen in your mind, and picture yourself doing the exercises with a smile and a feeling of relaxation in your body. When you have completed the exercises you will be able to continue your work in a more relaxed way thinking about something really pleasant in your life.

You can do these exercises in a lying or sitting position. Be sure you are comfortable. Maybe you need to remove a tight belt or your shoes. If you are sitting up, use a straight-backed chair and feel a string tugging the top of your head. This will straighten and stretch your spine. As an alternative you can bend your neck and allow your head to rest near your chest. You can initially feel the pull of your neck and shoulder muscles, but this will become easier as you do the exercises. Try both positions and see which one is best for you. If you are lying down have your legs slightly apart, put your arms down by your sides, palms down, fingers resting apart and elbows slightly out. Choose to do this exercise when you will have minimum disturbance and a reasonable amount of time. When you have practised you will find that you are able to do these exercises for short periods at work by taking 10 minutes off, leaving your

desk and going somewhere quiet for a few moments. Remember when you have done them you will deal better with your workload. The most important thing is to observe passively what is happening to your mind and body. Allow relaxation to happen, do not try to force it.

Begin your exercise by taking a deep breath and exhaling. You may choose to review the thoughts in your mind at that time and then let them go. Repeat your favourite word to yourself to describe relaxation:

I am at ease
I am at peace
I am relaxed
I am letting go

THURSDAY

Start by giving a message to your arms: 'My right arm is heavy, my right arm is heavy, my right arm is heavy. My left arm is heavy, my left arm is heavy, my left arm is heavy.' Say these words slowly, allowing yourself as much time as you need. Be pleased when you start to feel heaviness in your arms.

Proceed to your legs repeating the message: 'My right leg is heavy, my right leg is heavy, my right leg is heavy. My left leg is heavy, my left leg is heavy, my left leg is heavy.' Be pleased with the heaviness in your legs.

Say to yourself: 'My neck and shoulders are heavy, my neck and shoulders are heavy, my neck and shoulders are heavy.' Take a deep breath and exhale.

Repeat the message to yourself: 'My arms are heavy, my legs are heavy, my neck and shoulders are heavy.'

Continue by giving the message to the muscles in your arms: 'My right arm is warm. My right arm is warm. My right arm is warm. My left arm is warm. My left arm is warm. My left arm is warm.' Be aware of the blood running pleasantly and easily right through your whole body.

Allowing your legs to let go, say to them: 'My right leg is warm. My right leg is warm. My right leg is warm. My left leg is warm. My left leg is warm. My left leg is warm.' Continue breathing naturally and easily.

Move your mind to your neck and shoulders: 'My neck and shoulders are warm. My neck and shoulders are warm. My neck and shoulders are warm.'

Talk to your heart: 'My heartbeat is calm and regular. My heartbeat is calm and regular. My heartbeat is calm and regular.'

Slow your breathing by saying: 'My breathing is calm and regular. My breathing is calm and regular. My breathing is calm and regular'.

Concentrating on the tummy area: 'My tummy is warm and calm. My tummy is warm and calm. My tummy is warm and calm.'

Move to your forehead: 'My forehead is cool and calm. My forehead is cool and calm. My forehead is cool and calm.'

Now you have gone right through your body and you are ready to return to your normal state of awareness. Say to yourself, 'I am feeling calm and alert. I am feeling calm and alert. I am feeling calm and alert.'

Slowly open your eyes, stretch and sit or lie quietly for a few moments to adjust to the outside world.

Try these exercises for some weeks in order to progress into a state of complete calmness. Every time you do the exercises your body is one step nearer learning for itself how good it feels to be in a relaxed state. The more you do the exercises the more your body responds.

Conclusion for Thursday

Today we have asked you to further develop your own personal internal awareness by looking at all the things that give you pleasure and enhance your life. Listening to music can contribute to a more relaxed approach to life and encourage you to develop your imagination and creativity, rather than relying on television for passive entertainment. Finally, to complement this mental approach, we have introduced you to autogenic training which can enhance your awareness of your physical body.

FRIDAY

WELCOME TO FRIDAY

You are now moving towards the weekend and have a wide range of new approaches available to enable you to choose to look at your lifestyle from different angles. Some of the ideas and approaches may not relate specifically to you, so select those which are relevant and enjoyable.

You may like to use some of your energy planning how to use your time most effectively this weekend.

Today we set out the following ideas:

- Time management
- Interruptions and solutions
- Brilliant ideas notebook
- Living for the moment
- Taking risks
- Listening to the sound of your voice
- Instant relaxation
- Mirror watching
- Visualisation of a famous person
- Visualisation for Winter
- Relaxation from feet to head

We hope you enjoy Friday and that it helps you to plan and look forward to your weekend.

Time management

Most people are aware that they never have enough time but are so busy they cannot stop long enough to look at what they are doing every day. If they do stop they feel the whole routine might grind to a halt and the heavy load they carry might never be picked up again. Other people are able to put down their burden, put it in the dustbin and go through their life with lightness of heart, mind and spirit. Walk along the tightrope of life with all your energy going into each creative moment.

If you haven't completed the job you set out to do between 8.00am and 8.15am then the rest of the day need not be total chaos. What time management does is enable you to see what is really important to you in your life so you are able to deal with it. From the first moment you decide to look at what you are capable of achieving in a day, and how you are going to do it, you are looking at a new and positive you. You have given some time to yourself and looked at what is important in your life. There are 24 hours in every day, some of which you will spend in restful sleep or relaxation, but how will you spend the rest of your time?

FRIDAY

There is always more than one way of doing something, and after some relaxation your mind and body will be in a better position to work out which way is best for you. Why not start your problem solving by getting a large, thick sheet of paper? Perhaps you might like to pin it on the wall. Put the headings day, week and month and then brainstorm what situations, under the above headings, are likely to overwhelm you. Go through the list again and identify which are important, urgent, non-important. Learn to differentiate between urgent and important. Just because something is urgent doesn't necessarily mean it's important to you – and what is urgent to one person may be entirely unimportant to another. You can choose what priorities you give to things. Put your tasks on the list and rearrange it so as one goes on you take one task off it altogether. With any luck you may never need to do some tasks at all because they aren't really necessary or someone else will do them for you.

You may be surprised, having carried out this exercise, how much you can reduce the pressure on yourself by recognising in writing, rather than thoughts, the way forward to a more productive and rewarding future. Try it!

Remember the mind is the busiest part of the body so by introducing these new ideas you may be able to reduce the thought traffic to a tolerable level, giving you freedom, choice and space to enjoy more pleasurable and calmer thought patterns.

Personal circle exercise

We now offer you another time management exercise where you draw 'me' in the middle of a circle. Around 'me' you draw another circle showing what requires your immediate attention. Then around the outside of the circle, draw people and tasks that are not immediate but still there. You can decide what percentage of your time you are able to give to all the outside influences allowing a special time for 'me'. You can start by working on managing mornings, possibly allocating some tasks at work or at home to other people. The programme will enable you to structure your day so at the end of it you can look at yourself with pride and affection and not frustration and anger which wastes the energy you do have. When you have achieved a morning which is right for you then you can do a programme for the afternoon and evening.

Ideas diary

Something else you could try to help you manage your time is to get yourself a diary that shows the whole week. Start by noting down how you spend your time now. Write down when you get up and when you go to bed. Are these the right times for you? Would it benefit you to go to bed earlier or later? Write down how much time you spend travelling,

FRIDAY

how much time you spend at home. How much time do you want to give yourself? How much time do you want to give to other people? When you have worked out your present daily patterns, choose to give yourself half-an-hour a week to plan what your short and long-term goals are.

Short-term goals

In this allocated thinking time, write out what you intend to do each day. If you need to make some telephone calls, when is the best time to make them? If you need to buy some food, when is the best time to do so? List what items of food you need. They are better written down where you can see them, rather than floating round in your mind hoping to be discovered at the right time and the right place and not just after the shops have closed. Write down a manageable list of what you want to accomplish each day. Give yourself some praise when you have completed the list.

Long-term goals

Looking further ahead, you could put dates of birthdays, anniversaries and dates for paying bills in your diary. Are you someone who has difficulty in paying for the TV licence, or electricity or gas bills? Why not buy saving stamps on a regular basis? You could put in your diary the day you intend to purchase them. When the postman delivers the bills you will be able to relax and be pleased with yourself that you already have the money to pay.

Next, would you like to go through your year and plan visits or treats for yourself? These need not be expensive and you will then have built in something relaxing to look forward to rather than getting into the habit of saying 'I never have time for "me"'.

FRIDAY

Interruptions and solutions

Many times when you are working from your lovely lists or plans you will be subject to interruptions. The telephone will ring or you realise that a more urgent job needs doing than the one on your list or your favourite programme is on the television.

Solutions

Put yourself first when you are interrupted. What do *you* want to do? If the telephone rings, you could be brave, answer it yourself and say 'I am busy now. Can I ring you back at 8.00pm.' Put it on your ever present list.

Practise saying in front of the mirror 'The world will not end if I miss my favourite television programme'. You may need to repeat this several times. Cross off your favourite television programme from the list and do some relaxation or go for a nice walk. If you have a video, record your programme for viewing at a more convenient time.

Give yourself some praise for remembering your urgent task. With the difference between urgent and important in mind, decide whether you wish to deal with this task now or slot it into your list to be dealt with at a more appropriate time.

Brilliant ideas notebook – for your benefit

Always have with you a notebook and pen or pencil so whatever brilliant idea you have can be written down. Writing ideas on pieces of paper result in you searching under piles of newspapers, in rubbish bins and under the bed, usually with little success. An immediately accessible book of brilliant ideas is almost as good as winning the pools! You can include books you've heard about that you want to read, pieces of music you like, places you'd like to visit.

FRIDAY

People who work hard to achieve a personal goal and feel successful are likely to be exhilarated rather than exhausted. Always choose to be pleased with what you have done, not annoyed with yourself for what you haven't done. The more you are pleased with this unique person, 'you', the more this 'you' will feel inspired to welcome a new day, a new week, a new year with a feeling of 'I can handle it'.

Have you read through the paragraph half-heartedly saying to yourself 'I've heard it all before. I'm not capable of re-organising my life. I don't suppose it would make any difference'? Can you ask the part of you that is saying those words to consider whether they are beneficial to you? Would that part of you consider keeping a book of brilliant ideas or even slightly brilliant ideas for a day, a week, a month? Can you sit down for a moment, count from 10 to one and allow your body to become more relaxed with each number you count? Visualise, think or feel how you will start your book. What colour pen will you use? Where will you keep your book? What is the best time of day for you to write in it?

Living for the moment

One of the key elements of successful time management is living for the moment – putting your energy into what you have decided to do now and not worrying about the tasks you have allocated time to in the future. On a personal note, I choose to write my book in the garden today. The day is sunny and warm and I am sitting in a comfortable deckchair. Our new kitten is in the garden for the first time and is full of amazement at this incredible world. He feels his fur being ruffled by the wind and every inch he moves there is a new and exciting smell to be explored. He touches the grass for the first time. He sees an insect – is it to eat or to play with? It won't play and he doesn't like its taste so he disdainfully ignores it. He hears the wind and a strange object rushes towards him in the breeze. Will it attack? Should he bang it with his paw or sniff it?

He puts everything into exploring his surroundings, playing games, washing himself, eating and just flopping. If you pick him up when he is drowsy he is extremely heavy and floppy. In the waking state he has boundless energy and interest in life. Then he flops and gives all his attention to sleeping to regain his energy. This morning has been an exciting one for both of us as I anticipate what will happen next in the life of the kitten acknowledging his freedom of choice and lack of responsibility.

As human beings some of us have completely lost the art of relaxing after putting all our energies into whatever we are doing. I could be sitting in the garden not writing the book, a piece of paper in front of me and my mind on the weeding, the planting. If I was indoors I could be thinking about the cleaning, the shopping or the dinner. However, I have chosen to live in the world of **now** where the wind blows, the sun shines, the kitten plays, my husband is happy, the book is being written and all things are wise and wonderful.

Having had such a truly uplifting morning, no doubt later on the vacuum cleaner will be wielded and the garden weeded. However, it is possible that I may spend the afternoon watching the flight of the birds, the bees buzzing and the kitten walking in his brave new world. Why don't you try living for the moment?

Taking risks

Do something you have never tried before. This could range from changing your brand of toothpaste to going out to the Bahamas for a fortnight, depending on your personal circumstances. If you cannot afford the Bahamas then take yourself there in a visualisation.

Choose to have more successes than failures. For some people success may be getting up in the morning, washing themselves and getting into their clothes. For others it may be a well-paid job, an expensive car and a large home. Decide for yourself what success is to you, you don't have to accept how everyone else defines it. What each person needs is a sense of satisfaction and the wonderful feeling that they have done well. See each day of your life as an opportunity to succeed. Offer yourself a smile or share it with someone else, play yourself pleasant music in a traffic jam, brighten your office with a bunch of flowers.

Listening to the sound of your voice

When you are writing your diary, read out something you have written and listen to the sound of your voice. Have you ever thought what a wonderful instrument your voice is? If you are able to use your voice in a pleasant, natural and relaxed way, this is beneficial to your whole being. Knowing that the way you speak on the telephone is pleasant for someone to listen to makes it a good experience for both the speaker and the listener. If you are talking to someone who is angry or upset, they will feel calmed by the good sound of your voice. Talking slowly and with feeling is reassuring to listen to both for yourself and other people.

In many cultures people enjoy singing and chanting. It helps them to breathe and exercise their lungs. It is good for them to see other people enjoying the same experience. Would it be possible to get a group of friends together to enjoy singing or reading a play, or could you do it with your family? Could you all choose to sing along to a tape or a record? You may be pleasantly surprised by the amount of pleasure that this experience gives you.

FRIDAY

Talking or singing clearly and well does not necessarily mean loud. Maybe when you are in your car or bath you can sing or speak using the full power and pleasure of your lungs to practise singing slowly and clearly, listening to the beautiful sounds that you have the gift of making. Try to sing from your tummy – it will help the air reach the lowest part of your lungs and will aid your breathing exercises. Indulge all your senses in the song. An example of this is the opening sequence from *The Sound of Music* in which the beautiful scenery and emotive words conjure a magical experience for many people. Use your own favourite visual image which represents to you peace, calm and tranquillity. Enhance the visual image by introducing your favourite piece of music. Then allow yourself within this experience to sing your favouritee song as loud as you want which will enable you to refresh yourself in mind and body.

If there are voices talking to you in your mind, make sure that they are pleasant voices that are easy for you to listen to. The messages your mind wishes to give you can be spoken in a soft and comforting manner.

FRIDAY

To increase the capabilities of your voice try the following exercises, if possible alone, as you may be making a considerable amount of noise.

Exercise for the voice

Look in the mirror and stand with your feet apart. Imagine you are a tall tree with roots that go far down into the earth. It is best to have your knees flexible so that you are able to sway gently. If you stand still, you will stiffen both the voice and the body. Remember, shoulders relaxed, neck relaxed, jaw relaxed. As you become more used to looking at yourself in the mirror you can observe what position your body is in.

Imagine there is a string gently lifting the crown of your head up and away from your body. Allow your head to be centred, not tilted forward or back. Your neck and windpipe should feel free and ready to open for this lovely voice to come out.

Open your mouth as wide as you can. Stroke your cheeks just to feel if there is any tension. Draw your upper and lower lips tightly over your teeth with your mouth slightly open as you breathe in. As you breathe out, allow your mouth to return to a comfortable position, letting go of any tension. Breathing in through your nose and out through your mouth, you will become aware of the experience of breathing. As you breathe out you may notice your lips will close slightly. Experiment with breathing in and out with your mouth open and notice how this feels. When you yawn and open your mouth wide, it is because your body has decided you need more oxygen. Open your mouth fully from time to time and allow yourself to do some breathing exercises in the way we have described. As you continue to look in the mirror, purse your lips. You may feel a little funny doing these exercises so enjoy having a laugh at yourself.

Relax your jaw if it feels tight. Keeping your head reasonably still move your lower jaw around into different shapes, still watching yourself in the mirror. See if your jaw feels more comfortable when you have returned it to its normal position.

Tell your throat it is opening wide and say one or two things to yourself, noticing how your mouth is moving, and how you are breathing as you talk. Start singing one of your favourite songs, you may have already written down the words. Whether you sing the song well is unimportant. For this exercise you are focusing on the sound and on your breathing. As you sing louder does your mouth open wider and do you become more conscious of the sound coming through your open mouth? How does this feel? Continue by closing your eyes and seeing whether this creates any change in the quality of your voice. Sing as loud as you can and in doing so see if you can release any tension that may be affecting you both physically and mentally. Gradually, with your eyes open or closed, whichever you prefer, reduce the sound to a whisper and allow your arms and hands to relax and quietly reflect on how your voice affects your feelings.

FRIDAY

Instant relaxation

Another surprisingly effective, speedy relaxation exercise is to select a word which symbolises relaxation for you like peace, tranquillity or love, and shout the word in your mind. Repeat this word six times, each time reducing the volume of your voice until it finally becomes a whisper.

Having experienced this process repeat the exercise. This may produce a feeling of becoming more peaceful and relaxed. This exercise can be done alone or with people and can be very reassuring and rewarding.

Mirror watching

Here are some points that are helpful when looking into a mirror. Don't stand too close to it. You are there to observe the whole of your body so you need to be sufficiently far away to see your head and your feet at one time. As you stand there be comfortable with yourself. Look in the mirror, feel your face and observe how you look to yourself. If you are frowning remember that it takes more muscles to frown than to smile, so smile at yourself. Does this change how you feel? Let your eyes travel from the top of your head to the tips of your toes. Are your hands curled up or are they flexible and uncurled. How do your feet look? Do you feel if you make them slightly wider apart this creates a change for you? How do your shoulders look? For a moment just stand and look at yourself sideways. It is easier to see if your shoulders are tense by looking from the side. Notice how your breathing is, is your chest rising and falling? Is your stomach moving in and out? Do your shoudlers lift? Now consciously, still from the side, slow your breathing down and notice whether you experience any physical or mental relief.

When you are facing the mirror shake your hands to loosen them up. When you are standing sideways try lifting your shoulders and feeling the tension in your shoulders, neck and chest, which may make it difficult for you to breathe easily and naturally. As you breathe out become aware that your fingertips may feel lower down your legs, and your neck may feel slightly longer. When you return to facing the mirror notice whether you feel more at ease and comfortable standing in your original position.

At the end of the mirror exercise we would like you to tense every muscle as you breathe in, tighten your body, screw up your face and clench your fists. Then, very slowly, release every muscle, nerve and fibre and become aware of the difference.

Every time you look in the mirror renew your acquaintance with yourself. You may feel more comfortable and positive about the person you are looking at because you are giving that person permission and time to think about themselves. There are times when we need to say 'What about me,' to those around us.

Here is another exercise that you can do with your mirror.

Swing to relax

Stand in front of the mirror and sway your hands backwards and forwards creating the sensation and image of your hands moving in slow motion. Recognise that this particular exercise doesn't require a great deal of energy. As you do this, do you feel that you are placing more weight on your feet? Does it help you to stand more evenly? Increase the movement until you reach waist level with the forward movement of your hands. Then start turning your body from left to right in a swinging movement, allowing your arms and hands to be relaxed and easy. Study the movement and tell your hands to become heavier, then feel like the pendulum of a clock and make nice even movements. Flex your knees slightly and observe how this affects the rest of your body. What is your normal stance? Place your weight on your left foot and gently shake your right foot. Place your weight on your right foot and gently shake your left foot. Stand quietly allowing your body to be still and check in the mirror that your body looks relaxed and comfortable. Give yourself a smile for completing the exercise.

FRIDAY

Visualisation of a famous person

Now you have worked really hard on your mirror exercises reward yourself by having fun with some more visualisation.

As we know, our minds are under-used. This next piece is to enable your mind to enter the world of fantasy and create feelings and experiences that may surprise and delight you. Remember that some people think in words, some in pictures and some in feelings. For instance, if we asked you to see in your mind a red car, some people would see a red car, some people would have the words 'red car' in their mind, and some people would feel as if they were in a red car. Being aware of this will allow your mind to interpret each visualisation in your own unique way.

So, again getting yourself as comfortable as possible and taking five deep breaths, allow your mind to select a particular famous person. This can be someone you have seen in a film, read about or may have learned about at school. Build up a clear, bright picture of this person or see the words you have read about them or feel the feelings this person might have had. You may find it easy to be this person in your mind, or you may prefer to observe the person on a screen like a film.

What would you be wearing? How would your hair look? What sort of food would you eat? What would your life be like? How would your home be lit, heated and furnished? Who are your family and friends? Remember to breathe deeply and to continue this exercise for as long as you want. When you decide to conclude the experience let the picture slowly fade from your mind, knowing that you can return to see your 'home movie' whenever you want to. Learning to take your mind on a fantasy journey through time and space is fascinating to be able to do.

FRIDAY

When the image has faded, think about the room you were in when you started the exercise and construct a picture of it in your mind. Slowly open your eyes returning to the real world refreshed and surprised by the fantasy your wonderful mind is able to create. The more you ask your mind to look at positive experiences the more you will be able to go forward in life in a meaningful way. If one of your childhood dreams was becoming an actor or actress then try out the dream. If you find you are successful you can always join your local amateur dramatic company!

Visualisation for Winter

Here is a second visualisation for you to experiment with. See, feel and hear the scene and make it just right for you.

FRIDAY

Imagine that winter has a special quality and is a restful time where nature slows down and hibernates until spring comes round again. The days are short, the nights are long and you enjoy the pleasure of getting into a nice warm bed with soft covers, a firm mattress and the comfort of a hot water bottle.

You wake one morning to realise that overnight the frost and snow have come and you marvel at the world outside your window. All is crisp and white as if someone had touched everything with a sparkling magic wand. You open your window in sheer joy and take a handful of snow from your windowsill. How does it feel to you? Try touching your face with it and feel your skin tingle and glow. Put some on your tongue and taste it. You long to rush outside in warm clothes and be a child again, hearing your voice ringing in the cold frosty air.

You decide to walk to a nearby lake. As it is still early your footprints are the only ones to be seen and you feel like a mysterious snowman as you make no sound on the soft snow. You breathe deeply and swing your arms and walk briskly up a hill, knowing that when you reach the top you will be able to see the view right down to a lake at the bottom. You are aware of birds singing and in your pocket you have bread for the ducks on the lake. As you teach the top of the hill you anticipate the feeling you will have when you first see the lake and the surrounding trees all covered in sparkling white snow. As you reach the top the sight is magnificent and your mind drinks in the picture of white trees, white fields and the large lake with a coating of frosted ice on its surface. A small patch of water is still visible and you watch the ducks patiently waddling towards the water. The sheep in the fields have thick winter coats and are huddled against the white hedgerows. Together with the ducks and the birds, these are the only objects in your scene that have colour and movement and you enjoy watching their slow progress.

FRIDAY

You run down the hill slipping, sliding and shouting at the sheer pleasure of the scene. You throw your bread to the ducks and turn to retrace your footprints in the snow. Your stomach tells you that it needs some breakfast and you anticipate returning to your warm snug home, making some tea and preparing a warm nourishing meal. Perhaps you will come out again later and make a snowman or throw some snowballs.

Relaxation from feet to head

We end this chapter with another relaxation for you to experience. Try it and see how you feel.

I now relax every muscle in my body . . . The toes on my right foot are limp and relaxed. This feeling of relaxation is going all the way through the right foot to the ankle and my whole foot is limp and relaxed. Now I relax the toes on my left foot. This feeling of relaxation is going all the way through the left foot to the ankle and my whole foot is limp and relaxed.

FRIDAY

A feeling of heaviness and warmth slowly moves up the calf of my right leg so I am relaxed from my toes to my knee. I now allow the same pleasant feeling to move up the left calf so I am relaxed from my toes to my knee.

The feeling of warmth and heaviness spreads through the thigh muscle in my right leg so my right leg is relaxed right up to the hip and then my left thigh muscle relaxes so both feet and legs are limp, relaxed and heavy.

My eyes are heavy and drowsy. They are so relaxed they just want to close.

I am relaxing the fingers of my right hand. They are heavy and limp. My right hand is relaxing more and more. Now the muscles of the fingers of my left hand are letting go, the fingers are limp and relaxed. My left hand is relaxed and heavy. I allow that feeling to flow up my arms, the right forearm is heavy, the left forearm is heavy, the right upper arm is heavy, the left upper arm is heavy, both my hands and my arms are relaxed and heavy. This wonderful feeling flows up into my shoulders and I am bathed in a pleasant glow of relaxation.

At this time I am going to take three deep breaths. Each time I exhale my body will relax more and more. I breathe in and I breathe out giving full attention to my breathing. Each muscle in my chest, shoulders, back, tummy and hips is completely relaxed and my whole body is limp and heavy, limp and heavy.

I am now completely relaxed and my arms and legs are heavy and warm. My eyes are heavy, my head is heavy and all tension is released from my muscles. My jaw muscles are relaxed and my teeth are slightly apart. All the muscles in my face and scalp are limp and lazy and it is a wonderful feeling.

Conclusion for Friday

At the start of Friday we focused on how you can use your time and make it work for you. You can also make your voice work for you and have a positive influence both on yourself and those around you. Finally, we hope the visualisations we offered you further helped you to improve your imaginative qualities and widen your perspective of life.

When you turn the page the weekend will have arrived.

SATURDAY

WELCOME TO SATURDAY

Our introduction today assumes that you may have extra time at the weekend. We recognise that some of our readers may work at weekends so please adjust your time and space accordingly.

We would like you to reflect on what changes you have already made and those which you may be considering for the weekend and the following week. We offer a number of fairly short sequences for you to try and conclude by focusing on colour and its potential for you.

- Positive you
- Productive thinking
- Productive memories
- Positive results from negative feelings
- Taking control
- **Do it** sequence
- Breathing and eye closure exercises
- Tension relieving exercises for the head and neck
- Relaxation check
- Visualisation of an animal
- Experiment with colour
- Colour breathing

Positive you

Choose to make a list of positive things about yourself, for example:

I am a happy person and all good things will come to me.

I like other people and they like me.

I am unemployed and this gives me time to rethink my life.

I do my job as well as I am able.

There are many things in life that I find enjoyable.

I am a satisfied and contented person.

People see me as calm and reassuring.

Switch to the positive channels of your mind. Learn the positive pathways to take which may have become cul-de-sacs in your mind through the experiences which life has presented to you. It is easy to think negative thoughts but you do have the ability to create positive ones. Here is a useful poem for you to read:

To think bad thoughts is the easiest thing in the world,
If you leave your mind to itself it will spiral down into unhappiness,
To think good thoughts requires effort, so train your mind to dwell on
Sweet perfumes, the touch of silk, tender rain drops on flowers
The tranquillity of the dawn.

James Clavell, Shogun

Maybe you would like to copy out the poem, frame it and hang it on the wall.

Productive thinking

Having worked on some positive thoughts about yourself, you can develop your productive thinking. There are many things you may wish to ask yourself.

Who are you? What do you want? What is the real world? What are your beliefs? Do your daydreams need to be limiting and unhappy or can they be more positive?

Have you experienced achievement and satisfaction in your life? What was the most satisfying experience you have ever had? Would you like to repeat it? Ask other people what their most satisfying experience was and how they achieved it.

What is satisfaction?

What is achievement?

Are you satisfied with most things you do? Some of the things you do? None of the things you do? Why? How can you be a satisfied person? What do you need in your life for satisfaction?

Can you wake up every day expecting to have a satisfactory and enriching day? Can you get out of bed and tell yourself you feel wonderful? If you have a pain or an ache somewhere, remind all the other parts of your body that they feel good. Tell the painful part that it will soon feel easier and more comfortable.

Send messages to all the other parts of your body thanking them for the comfortable feelings they are giving to you. Your mind and body like to hear cheerful messages.

Who will choose to make you well?
Who will choose to make you happy?
Who will choose to make you contented?
Who will choose to make you satisfied?
You will!

Who will choose to make you gloomy?
Who will choose to give you a headache?
Who will choose to make you late for work?
Who will choose to make you feel anxious?
You will!

If you don't choose to look after and love yourself, how can anyone else look after and love you? How can you look after and love anyone else?

You are whoever you choose to be. Sometimes in life we become sick and weary because we have let our energy level become low. We have taken on too many burdens. We have worked too many long hours. We feel too much guilt and suffering. All these feelings are created by the person inside you and they can be changed. This one unique person is creative and able to look at a lot of different choices. Your whole life is created by the choices you make, so think carefully at each stage of it. When you are an old person it would be nice to look back at the young person with delight and happiness. Being an old person can be fun if you are able to look back at the young and middle-aged person in a positive way.

An 'if only' person is created as a child and can still be an 'if only' person at 90, even if they are a millionaire. In this case they would probably say if only I had two million. Put love and laughter into your own life and you put it into everyone else's as well.

SATURDAY

Productive memories

Here is an exercise for you to choose to practise experiencing feelings of satisfaction and achievement. The more you practise and strengthen feelings of satisfaction and achievement, the more you can apply them to your life.

So, sitting comfortably, take five deep breaths and drift back in time to when you achieved something that was really worthwhile, something that meant a great deal to you at the time. It could have been doing a drawing at school, passing a test, making a friend. Quietly choose to drift back to an achievement in your childhood. Choose to get in touch with the excitement, the pleasure, the joy you felt at the time. The 'I can do it' feelings. Let these feelings grow stronger and stronger. Go through the whole sequence as if you are watching a film you really enjoy. Make it colourful and interesting and maybe put in some music from that time. Finally, allow the film to fade away and be pleased that you allowed yourself to feel so good. Let yourself use these feelings every day. They are your own special feelings and will add greatly to your enjoyment and relaxation.

SATURDAY

Positive results from negative feelings

This is another exercise that you can choose to do to counteract any negative thoughts and feelings that you may have.

Extend your arms out straight, palms facing towards each other about four inches apart. Imagine a rubber band around your wrists holding them near to each other. This rubber band represents any negative thoughts and feelings you have about yourself that keep you from feeling good. Say to your hands that they are now able to move away from each other. There is a positive force pulling, tugging. Notice as you pull your hands apart that there is a satisfying sound as the rubber band breaks and frees you from all negative thoughts and feelings. Now you can rest your hands comfortably. Again search in your past for a positive, satisfying experience. We have all had this kind of experience, as far back as learning to walk or sitting up. In your imagination enjoy the positive experience and see your life as a succession of positive experiences waiting to be enjoyed.

Taking control

Can you look at life as a long road? Sometimes you can be travelling along a motorway with no hold-ups, other times there is a 12-mile tailback. Use the traffic jams in your life to create stories, take an interest in the people around you, play some music. You can't do anything to control the traffic jam, so use the opportunity to assess the areas of your life where you do have control and decide where you are going from here. When you do this, uncomfortable experiences do not have the same meaning.

Are you the kind of person who has a bad headache on Tuesday, is late for work on Wednesday and is tired out on Thursday? Can you write a new scenario for yourself where unexpected and pleasant thoughts occur which change the meaning of Tuesday, Wednesday and Thursday.

You could give yourself the message 'My headache is there to tell me that I am becoming stressed and over-anxious. I will take time to listen to a relaxation tape and I will visualise my head as being more comfortable'. Ask your headache if it isn't ready to go could it be more comfortable in, say, two hours.

Think about the other two examples of being late for work on Wednesday and tired on Thursday. Do you have a pattern of behaving in a certain way each day? Can you alter the pattern? Take a long cool look at the problem you have chosen to deal with in whatever way is best for you. Knowing you have decided to take control will be a relaxing and rewarding experience.

'Do it' sequence

Throughout this book, we have encouraged you to try exercises and choose to do those that work best for you. If you find you are overwhelmed at making changes to your daily routine, select only one exercise at a time. If you find it difficult to choose, you could look at the book at random and pick out the first one you find, or look at the back which gives you the whole range to choose from and the amount of time needed for each exercise or visualisation.

Sometimes we get stuck when we try to think what to do. The most important thing is to **do it**. These words can give you a feeling of excitement and determination to become a **do it** person. If you need to make an important decision, **do it**. If it is the wrong decision, you can make changes afterwards, but if you never make the decision at all you are left with the fear of not being able to make a decision, your mind in chaos and other decisions looming that you will be too frightened to make. Put **do it** signs all around you and remember to give yourself a mental pat on the back for making a decision.

SATURDAY

Breathing and eye closure exercise

This is a simple and effective exercise and once you have read it through slowly and carefully you will be able to go straight into the exercise without needing to refer to the instructions.

As you breathe in we want you to concentrate on keeping your eyes open and count from one to four. As you breathe out we want you to count from one to eight and let your eyes gently close. Continue opening your eyes as you breathe in and closing your eyes as you breathe out. You may notice a warm and comfortable feeling inside as you begin to let go both mentally and physically. The slower you breathe out the more difficult it is for you to open your eyes when breathing in. When you have reached the stage when it is easier to keep your eyes closed just enjoy a calm feeling for as long as you want.

Alternate nostril breathing

This is a soothing, calming exercise balancing the left and right hand sides of the body. It is pleasant if you can do this sitting on the floor, but if this is uncomfortable then sitting on a chair is fine. It is best if you can choose to sit upright with your shoulders relaxed. You may find that some gentle music assists you with this exercise.

Raise your right hand slowly and deliberately; use your thumb to close the right nostril and breathe in slowly through the left nostril. Close both nostrils with your thumb and forefinger for as long as it is comfortable, then, keeping the left nostril closed, exhale slowly through the right. Inhale through the right nostril, hold, and exhale through the left. Do this five times.

Did you manage to slow your breathing down? Did you have a soothing and calming feeling? Did you feel you had spent a few moments in a pleasant way? Is it hard for you to sit down without a paper or the television? You may like to go through the exercise again mentally counting to four when you breathe in, five as you hold and six as you breathe out. Are these pauses acceptable? If not choose which numbers are best for you.

Breathing and touching exercise

Here is another breathing exercise which you may like to do lying down on the floor or on the bed. As you lie down, notice each part of your body coming into contact with the surface you are resting on. When you are comfortable you can begin thinking about your breath being able to contact any part of your body. Each time you breathe in you send energy to a particular part of your body. Each time you breathe out you send a message of calmness and relaxation.

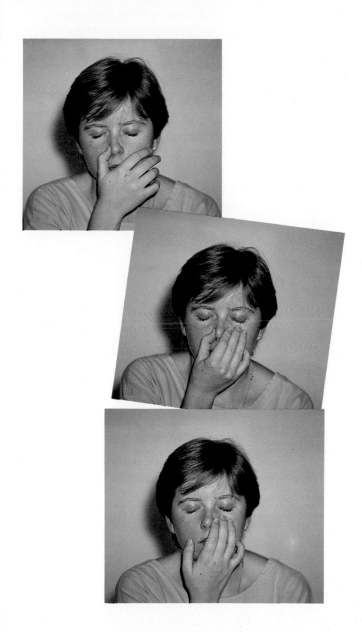

First, lightly rest the fingertips of both hands on your throat, breathe in and out several times focusing your breath on that area and saying to yourself: 'I am focusing my breath exactly where my fingertips are touching.' Next, move your fingertips gently down your body to the centre of your chest and focus your breathing there saying: 'I am focusing my breath exactly where my fingertips are touching.' Move your fingertips gently down to your solar plexus, which is just below the breast bone and focus your breathing there saying: 'I am focusing my breath exactly where my fingertips are touching.' Move your fingertips to just below your navel, focus your breathing there and say: 'I am focusing my breath exactly where my fingertips are touching.' Let your hands rest gently by your sides and visualise your breathing going right down to the tips of your toes.

Tension relieving exercises for the head and neck

For many of us tension in the neck and shoulders is very noticeable when we are making extra demands upon ourselves. This simple exercise may help you alleviate the symptoms or stop you from becoming tense in the first place. Remember you are unique, so choose your exercises with care. See what degree of success you have. What is best for you?

Neck rolling

To do this exercise you can sit comfortably in a chair or stand up.

Begin by concentrating on taking five deep breaths. As you breathe in roll your neck slowly and easily in slow motion to the right and then as you breathe out return your head to its normal central position. Breathing in again, allow your neck to roll to the left. As you breathe out return your head to its central position. Breathing in again gently and slowly allow your head to lower itself until your chin is nearly touching your chest. Return it to its normal position as you breathe out. Finally, breathe in and roll your head to the right, breathe out and roll your head to the left, then back to your normal central position. Repeat five times or more if you feel your neck and shoulders are still tense. Give yourself a moment at the end of the exercise to check how your mind and muscles are feeling. You may find that telling this part of your body that it is going to get warmer and warmer may enable the muscles to let go more effectively. Is it possible for you to do this exercise even more slowly next time?

Tapping exercise

Sitting comfortably in a chair or lying on a bed, using whichever hand you feel more comfortable with, very gently tap all over your scalp moving in whichever direction your mind takes you. This may enable your mind to listen to the tapping and give it something to focus on. Gradually work around the areas of your face, being very gentle with your tapping. Notice where there is any tension and gradually work around your eyes, down your cheeks, around your mouth, down your nose and into your neck. Then gently tap the backs of your hands with your fingers and then the inside of your fingers and thumbs. Tap around the palm of your hand and as you do so observe whether it is warm or cold. How do your fingers feel? Tell yourself that your hands will work perfectly for you if they are relaxed and comfortable.

Finally, breathing slowly and evenly, remind yourself that you can go at your own pace.

Relaxation check

Before we go on to our final visualisations for Saturday, we would like you to check through your body right now and notice how you feel. Are your arms and hands relaxed? Are your legs and feet relaxed? Take some deep breaths, uncross everything so you are not wasting energy, stand up and shake your arms and legs to reduce any tension and refresh yourself.

Circle of confidence

Build a circle of confidence around you, not a circle of fear and anxiety.

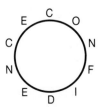   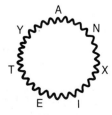

SATURDAY

Visualisation of an Animal

Now you have completed one or more of these calming down exercises you may choose to enhance your weekend by doing the following visualisation.

Can you choose to use your mind in a positive way by visualising yourself as an animal or a bird having the experience and freedom of being totally at one with nature? Maybe you can recall from a television documentary a particular animal or bird you are able to identify with. You may be surprised at the selection you make. At our evening classes when we ask people to relax by breathing deeply and allowing their minds to freewheel they have experienced the freedom of being an eagle soaring above the earth. One woman was a crocodile lying on the mud flats in the sun and lazily slipping in the water to refresh herself. Other people have chosen to be cats, lions or cheetahs using muscle power and strength in an economic way to run at full speed on a sunlit plain. You can choose any animal from any country you like.

Many people have been able to express their feelings in a positive way by choosing to forget their human identity for a short while. The feedback we get from our classes is often full of humour and thought-provoking. You may be surprised at how easy this exercise is. You may discover how exciting it is to be way up in the clouds or deep down in an ocean. So go ahead and have 10 minutes being any animal or bird you choose. Can you share your experience with a friend or relative and get them to experiment as well?

Does this experience offer you new insight that you can use in your daily life?

SATURDAY

Experiment with colour

Colour is very important in your life. Colour can create a physical and emotional reaction increasing your wellbeing. Miracle cures have been reported in cathedrals in olden times. These were attributed to the stained glass windows. As the sun came through the coloured glass, many ills were cured.

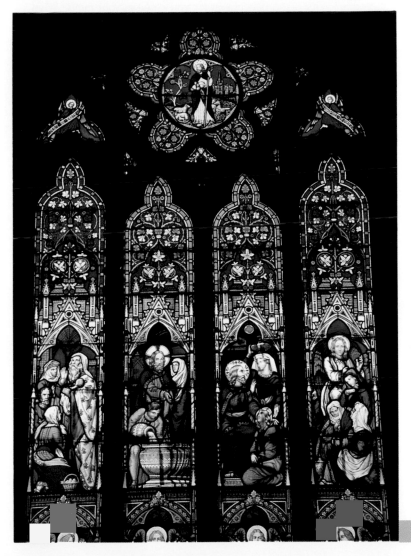

SATURDAY

What sort of colours do you choose to wear? To live with? What colour flowers do you like? How do you feel on a grey day? What is your favourite season, spring, summer, autumn, winter? What was your favourite colour as a child? What are your friends' favourite colours? How do you feel towards grey, blue, green, red, purple?

Do you see colours in your mind? Do you see different colours when you feel good to the colours you see when you feel sad? What is the difference? What is the best colour for you to see in your mind? What colour makes you feel happy? What colour makes you feel angry?

You can purchase light bulbs of different colours and experiment with the relaxation exercises bathed in a colour which you feel has a influence on your approach to life. Try it!

Throughout this book, we are attempting to help you create a new mental approach to your life. You can achieve a relaxed and comfortable lifestyle. Colour can make us feel good and positive. When we see a particular situation in our life which is colourful, then that colour can have an effect on our mental reaction and create good feelings in our body. The way we interpret colour is a mental experience and we would like you to experiment in whatever way is right for you. Your reaction to particular colours can also have a healing effect and generate more energy. Remember that black and white are colours. If your mind is black, can you change it to another colour? Remember the exercise on page 41? Just take a risk and look closely at a colour you have never studied.

We would now like to use colours in simple visualisations which will give you an opportunity to discover which colour can create an inner calm, and which colour can offer you energy.

Visualisation for orange

There is a village near us where the sun sets in brilliant orange over a sweeping landscape of fields of sheep and cows, hopfields and oast houses. To the right there is a small church. In the distance there is a line of trees. Sweeping around to the left, there is an old stately home. It is one of the longest summer evenings. As you close your eyes and create this image, place the orange sun at whatever point in the sky you want it. Watch this orange sun sink very slowly, bathing the whole scene in a gentle light which creates a dreamlike effect. You may notice that your eyelids flicker as you develop this scene. You may notice that your breathing is calmer as you watch the sun sink towards the horizon. You may equally feel that you are sinking deeper into a state of peace and tranquillity. As darkness falls reflect how the image of orange affected you and if your mind responded in a positive way.

SATURDAY

Visualisation for yellow

As you allow your mind to focus on the colour yellow perhaps you would like to draw a mental picture of the side of a hill. In your mind you can walk slowly towards a field, along a sunlit path, knowing that when you arrive you will be able to have a pleasant lie down in the field. As you get nearer to the field, you notice how peaceful it is and how the air around is shimmering on this perfect summer's day. As you reach the field and prepare to lie down you notice there is a profusion of yellow flowers which sway in a gentle breeze. You observe these lovely yellow natural flowers and spend some pleasant moments lost in admiration for all the wonders of nature that surround you. Maybe you can make a daisy chain or pick some buttercups just for you.

Visualisation for red

Can you visualise that you own the perfect country cottage which has a thatched roof, small painted windows and an oak front door which is always there waiting to welcome you? When you arrive at your cottage you notice that the front garden is alive with colour. Around your front door and all over your front garden are red roses which hold their faces up towards the sun. In your visualisation, if you want, the sun can always be shining. You have an old country wooden seat outside the front door of your cottage and you love to sit outside enjoying the fragrance and sight of these beautiful flowers.

Visualisation for green

Choose to go into an old-fashioned conservatory with a curved roof that is filled with plants and flowers of every description from tiny little violas to huge rubber plants. Ivies climb up the walls and your mind's eye sees all the different shades of green that nature has provided for you to look at. There is a comfortable rocking chair in the conservatory, and as you sit in it your body enjoys the gentle rocking motion. You feast your eyes on this natural scene of beauty.

Visualisation for blue

In this visualisation for blue we would like you to visit the Mediterranean. You can choose to walk around a natural rocky inlet feeling the warmth of the sun. You can look out into the blue bay where boats gently rock on the clear, crystal calm water. The bay is sheltered and you may choose to relax your body in the warm water, noticing how it feels as you swim among shoals of brightly coloured fish. You can hear the ripple of the water as your body disturbs it. All around you can see different coloured rock formations. Maybe you would like to float on your back, tasting the salt on your lips, hearing the sound of the water and feeling the warmth in this deeply peaceful and timeless cove.

Visualisation for indigo

Visualise yourself somewhere in a country where it is hot and exciting. The colours are bright and startling. The people are warm and friendly. There is always music and laughter. See yourself under an indigo blue sky at a barbecue on a beach. Join in the singing and dancing and enjoy the taste of the barbecued food. The clearness of the sky enables you to see the moon rise, the stars shine and the heavens produce their own nightly display for you to watch and enjoy. Feel the rhythms of the music. Let your whole mind and body be involved in this adventurous experience.

Visualisation for violet

Take yourself down a cobbled street hundreds of years ago. Fill your senses with all the sights, sounds and smells. This is a busy area of a city where all the traders are selling their wares. You can choose to buy fine fresh fish, colourful vegetables, meat, fruit, cottons, ribbons and lace. One of the most colourful sights to be seen in the streets is an old lady who is surrounded on all sides with bunches of violets tied with white ribbon and fresh with raindrops. You buy a bunch and receive a smile from the old lady. You put the bunch to your nose and inhale the deep fragrance and picture how the violets will look in a special vase at home.

Colour breathing

Another way of using colour is by an exercise called **colour breathing**. Get into a comfortable position and focus on your breathing. Introduce the colour you have selected very slowly, imagining you are breathing in this colour. If you want to you can visualise the colour floating around you and coming inside you. Observe the benefit you are experiencing both mentally and physically. Continue until you feel you are ready to move on to another colour and compare each colour so that you can harmonise colours in helping you relax in the future.

Did the colour fill every part of your body or just your arms and legs? Is it in your head? Can you see it around you? Is it a good feeling? Is it a relaxing feeling?

Conclusion for Saturday

How did you find what we offered you today? We have offered a fairly mixed weekend assortment for you to select from in your new approach to relaxation. Have you rated these exercises in order of priority? It may be that you choose to record your responses on the list at the end of the book for future reference. When you re-read this book you can then see immediately what are the most productive sequences for you.

SUNDAY

WELCOME TO SUNDAY

Now we have arrived at the final day and have pleasure in offering you the following ideas:

- New options for Sunday
- Progressive relaxation
- Recording your future progress
- Enjoying your food
- Candle watching
- Old house visualisation

New options for Sunday

See Sunday as a day of opportunity. How you are going to enjoy this full day of rest? For a moment just reflect on how traditional Sundays have been spent in recent times. What changes can you make to your Sunday? Are there things you would like to do but have not spared time for them? How are your Sunday evenings? Do they become overshadowed by the thought of Monday? Right up to the time you go to bed, offer yourself pleasant music, maybe a radio programme, a game of Scrabble or chess. Try something different that you don't normally do and see it as an adventure. Don't look back at failure – look forward to success.

Maybe today, when you have chosen from the options we have listed, you could also decide which exercises you are going to enjoy next week.

SUNDAY

Progressive relaxation

We have saved several exercises for Sunday which is a special day when you have more time. The major exercise we will be giving you today is Progressive Relaxation which is powerful and relaxing. This may also be a day when you can remind yourself about your senses of smell, taste, hearing, seeing and feeling.

We would now like you to make your usual preparation for relaxation. We are aware that to carry out these exercises you need to read and then remember with your eyes closed. Initially, it may be best for you to experiment with one small piece of the exercise at a time. Each time you may find it easier to picture yourself experiencing tensing and relaxing until, with practice, you are able to go through the whole exercise.

These exercises are to be enjoyed so have fun and tell yourself the more you practise the more you will benefit.

Exercise for progressive relaxation

To start with, we want you to breathe in and tense every muscle in your body beginning with screwing up your forehead, your eyes, your jaws, your hands, shrugging your shoulders as high as you can, tensing chest muscles, tummy muscles, hips, thighs, calves and screwing up your toes. As you breathe out, allow all these areas to relax and let go. In doing this remember that as you tell the different muscles to react you allow a little time in between each instruction so your mind can slow down and enjoy what it is doing.

Then, lying on a bed or sitting on a chair, we want you to gently close your eyes. Are there any images which spring into your mind? Do you want them there? If not, let them go. There may be thoughts crowding in asking you to feel guilty that you have devoted this time to yourself. Let them go. What do you hear around you? Is it something you can incorporate into your relaxation? If you stroke the surface you are resting on how does that feel to you? Many of us forget to use our senses. Take a moment to concentrate on hearing, touching and noticing how you are feeling at this time, recognising that you are allowing yourself to drift into a pleasant physical and mental experience. Distance yourself from any sounds that distract. Don't let them be part of your world at this time.

Now focus on your breathing and, without trying too hard, allow yourself to breathe naturally and easily. At the end of the exercise lie still and remain at peace for as long as you want. Do not allow the final instructions to influence feelings you are experiencing.

Focusing on your head breathe in slowly and wrinkle your forehead, count to four and then let go. As you breathe out count to four again if you find this number acceptable. During this particular experience you may notice your eyelids flickering as you concentrate. This is a normal response that can enhance the experience.

Focusing on your eye muscles breathe in slowly then screw them up as tightly as you can. As you do this you may notice some tension in your forehead. Hold that feeling for a count of four then slowly release the tension as you breathe out to a point where your eyes almost open. You may experience a feeling of relaxation spreading through the rest of your face.

Focusing on your mouth breathe in slowly clenching your teeth and lips and notice in your mind any tension in this area. Hold to a count of four, noticing if this tension extends to the back of your head. Breathe out and be pleased that you have decided to let go and focus on relaxing any tension.

With your mouth gently closed breathe in slowly, gently pushing your tongue up into the roof of your mouth. Hold to a count of four. Become aware of the tension in your lower face. As you breathe out, let your tongue return to a comfortable position. You may find that you feel more relaxed if you open your mouth slightly. Before you move on to other parts of your body, breathe in slowly and tense, as tightly as you can, the different parts of your face. Hold this for a count of four, then as you breathe out gently allow the tension to slip away.

Now focus on your shoulders. To start with, it might be necessary to become aware of whether you need to adjust your position to allow yourself to flex your shoulder muscles more freely. As you do this particular sequence you may notice tension in the back of your neck. Focusing on your shoulders breathe in slowly and push your shoulders

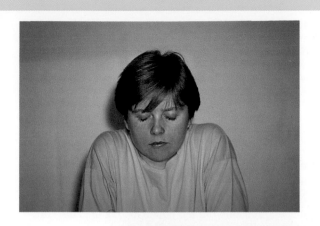

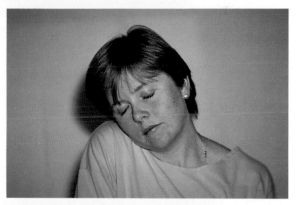

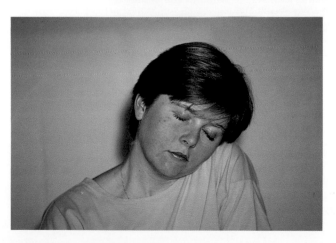

up towards your ears. Exaggerate the whole movement. Hold for a count of four. As you breathe out, let your shoulders drop and become aware that your neck may be slightly longer, which is a sign that you have let go of any tension. Well done! As you breathe in slowly, push your right shoulder up to your right ear, hold it for a count of four and then gently allow your right shoulder to slip back to a comfortable position as you slowly breathe out. Repeat with your left shoulder.

Breathe in slowly, push your arms straight up towards the ceiling and with your fists clenched notice your fingers pressing into the palms of your hands. Hold for a count of four, feeling the tension in your elbows. As you breathe out let your arms drop onto your lap with a satisfying slapping sound. This is a strong indication that you have removed tension from your arms and hands, and they feel wonderful.

As your hands continue to rest on your lap notice the material they are touching. Is it rough or smooth? Warm or cold? As you breathe in, slowly clench your hands and as you breathe out allow your fingers to slide down the surface they are resting on. Flick them up and down to remove any residual tension.

Remembering that breathing is an important part of relaxation, we are now going to spend a few moments focusing on this. Breathing in as slowly as you can, and filling your lungs with life-giving fresh air, notice the tension in the chest and rib cage, and that your shoulders have lifted. Hold for a count of four. As you let go of this deep breath, experience the sensation of your whole body sinking back to a comfortable position. Feel pleased that you have increased the amount of oxygen to your brain. Repeat slowly, take three deep breaths and then allow your breathing to return to its normal pattern.

Still focusing on your breathing, take a slow breath and arch your back. Hold for a count of four. Notice whether some parts are more tense than others. Breathe out slowly allowing each bone in your back to return gently and safely onto the resting surface. Repeat this exercise, allowing tension to decrease even more. This time when you have breathed out and returned your back to a normal resting position, check carefully through every muscle in your back giving them messages to let go. Focusing on your tummy muscles, breathe in slowly drawing them in towards the backbone. Hold for a count of four. Breathe out and slowly release the tummy muscles until they are in a comfortable position. Breathing in slowly, push out your tummy muscles as far as they will go. Hold to a count of four and allow your tummy to go back to a resting position as you breathe out.

Focusing on your hips and legs, press them down into the surface they are resting on as you breathe in slowly. Hold for a count of four and notice the tension in this area. Does the tension affect your tummy as well? Breathe out and allow your hips and legs to rest comfortably.

Lying quietly for a moment, spend time being really pleased with yourself for giving attention to all these parts of your body.

Focusing on your legs and breathing slowly, tense the calf muscles allowing this tension to spread into the knees and then the thighs. Hold this for a count of four and then breathe out, let go and rest comfortably. Focusing on your left foot curl the toes upwards towards your face as you breathe in. Hold for a count of four noticing any tension in your foot and your lower leg. Breathe out slowly and allow your toes to return to normal, wiggling them around to check all the tension has gone. Do the same with your right foot.

Breathing in slowly repeat the exercise, but this time curl both feet and all of your toes towards your face then allow your feet to become limp, loose and lazy.

Breathing in slowly, curl your left foot down and away from you. Hold the tension for a count of four and release it, again allowing your toes to enjoy a pleasant wiggle as you breathe out. Repeat the exercise with your right foot. When you are ready complete the exercise with both feet.

Quietly check through your whole body again to see if it is pleasantly comfortable.

To return to your normal waking state, count from one to 10 and slowly come back to full awareness. If you feel it is appropriate, have a slow stretch. Enjoy the good feelings that you have which will enable you to put renewed energy into your day. If you want to stay in this relaxed state please do so for as long as you like.

You have allowed yourself to communicate with the muscles of your body and you have asked them to become supple and relaxed. This conversation between mind and body is an enabling exercise which gives them the opportunity of working together in harmony. We need to offer our bodies love and affection, and pride in achievement because we are our own internal doctors and our bodies are willing to respond readily to positive messages from us.

Reflecting on this exercise, as with others in this book, you are learning to create inner health which will have a positive impact on your life, and will offset any negative outside influences. Many of us are so busy with our lives that we ignore our body's signals to slow down and take some care of ourselves. But you are able to choose to create inner calm and peace, which will give you the opportunity of finding life rewarding and pleasurable. Think about and notice the internal **you** who has intuition and insight.

Recording your future progress

It is important to remember that you need to read this book several times, and complete the exercises on a regular basis, to gain the most value from it. On each subsequent reading you may find you become interested in sequences which you didn't relate to initially. If you choose to change your life you do need to plan to consolidate a new attitude.

It may be of value to use your *Time Management* diary (see pages 63–64). You can then record in days, weeks and months the times which you plan to use to reinforce your new approach. Plan realistically, and use a red pen to highlight the times you intend to devote to yourself. In another colour pen, record what actually happened on those days, whether you were able to carry out the planned exercises and what benefits you gained from doing them. Choose to enjoy these periods of uncluttered time. You will find yourself better able to return to your normal tasks after spending some time on your relaxation programme.

Enjoy your food

We are going to mention food as a form of relaxation. So much has been said about what you should eat that choosing the 'right' food can become a source of stress. Scares about contamination can contribute to the fears we have about our food. But changing your diet completely can totally isolate you both inside and outside the family.

In some homes different members of the family eat at different times, in different places and very often all eating different meals! The pleasure of sitting down together, or on your own, to a simple meal is something to look forward to and cherish.

Can you make a plan of how, when and what you intend to eat and once you have got your plan, enjoy it? There are lots of books and other information to help you plan. Maybe in these days of stresses and strains, we need to enjoy our food in order to give us the energy to deal with each day. Maybe a large ice cream is something you need from time to time. If this is the case, don't feel guilty about it, enjoy it. You can bear in mind all the advice nutritionists give and eat a well-balanced diet, but you can still enjoy an occasional treat. Leave guilt off the meal table and eat your Sunday dinner with pleasure in mind. Give yourself time to relax and enjoy every mouthful.

Candle watching

Candle watching is a proven calming and pleasant way of spending time. Candle light is gentle, comforting and economical. It can give your room a sense of peace and tranquillity because the harshness of the light is dissolved. Artificial light is now being recognised as intrusive and 'full spectrum' bulbs are now available which are similar to sunlight.

We would like you to use candles which are safe and suggest nightlight candles which you can put on a heat-proof base. Think carefully about what colour you choose. Many shops stock candles that have attractive smells so again think carefully about your choice.

To do this exercise it is more satisfying sitting up than lying down. You can place the candle either on the floor or on a coffee table so that you are looking down at it. Decide exactly where you are going to sit. Your favourite piece of music in the background will help to create your own special atmosphere.

Having lit the candle in a safe and secure place, focus on your breathing and gently become aware of where your breath is going when it comes into your body, and how it feels when it returns through your nose. Look at how your body is resting. Is the chair you have chosen a comfortable one? Allow your head to be centred so that you have a clear view of the candle without causing any discomfort to your neck and shoulders. To start with, remember that your mind may wander. Try to concentrate on

the candle flame. What can you see? Is the flame flickering? Liken yourself to a candle flame which flickers as a result of external influences. If you protect the flame it very gently burns away using the minimum amount of energy. By carrying out this particular exercise, you are protecting yourself from external influences and reducing quite dramatically the amount of energy you use physically and mentally.

As you watch the flame, notice its colours. What shape is the flame? Does it burn at the same rate all the time? If you close your eyes, can you retain the image of the flame for 10 seconds? Is that a pleasant experience? Open your eyes and see how accurate your image was. We want you to repeat that process three times. Remember that you can spend as little or as long as you want training your mind to absorb the calmness of the candle flame.

If you still have time to spend in this way, completely concentrate on the flame and allow your eyelids to become heavier and heavier each time you breathe out to a point where your eyelids would be more comfortable if they were closed. If you can retain the image in your mind, that is fine. Remain in this comfortable position for as long as you want. Feel free at any time to go through the sequence again, using the candle flame as your point of concentration.

To end the sequence, we want you to open your eyes slowly and in your own time extinguish the flame, feeling a sense of accomplishment and wellbeing. Make a note in your diary or in your mind as to when you are going to repeat this enlightening experience.

Keep the candles and the matches in a special place so they are readily available when you next want to use them.

If you enjoy music, you may find the soft, subtle light of some candles may enhance the value of the music and of the composer for you. Try it. It could work for you – take the risk.

Old house visualisation

Use the amazing power of your mind with all your senses to create an experience which will provide a special place to go to at any time in the future. In this special place you can be at peace with yourself and your surroundings. You may surprise yourself by the rewards you can get from practising this particular exercise at regular intervals.

To start with, we want you to create an image, with your eyes either open or closed, of an old house. This old house could be one that you have visited at some stage or a figment of your imagination. Take yourself into the front garden of this house to enjoy the beauty all around you. Choose which time of year you want it to be. The garden provides you with a feeling of serenity as you admire the achievements of nature.

When you have spent some time in the garden, then you decide to add to your pleasure by looking at the inside of the house.

In a slow and leisurely manner you feel yourself walking into the house. Is it more comfortable with people around you or, on this particular day, do you want to be on your own?

Having walked into the front hall, slowly walk up the wide staircase and when you reach the tenth stair, turn around and survey the scene in your mind. Do you detect a particular smell related to this old house? If you reach out and touch the banisters, are they made of wood or brass? Is there carpet on the stairs? Can your mind's eye look around and see if there are pictures or portraits of the owners or their ancestors? How do these people look? What period of history could they have lived in? Are there dates on the pictures? Is there a beam of light coming from a high window creating a special patch of colour? As you look around, what sort of furniture or ornaments are down below you in the hall? Are there any beautiful vases or pots of flowers? You may be aware of the sound of a grandfather clock ticking in one corner of the hall.

Turn round and continue up the stairs until you reach the landing with creaky floorboards and small windows overlooking a cobbled courtyard. This courtyard has stables and you can imagine how the view must have looked when the house was first built. You can hear the jingle of harnesses and see the horses being groomed and prepared for people to ride out into the countryside.

The landing has several large oak doors which are closed, so you open one and look into a rather grand bedroom. This bedroom has a large four poster bed with a frilled canopy. Choose the colour of the canopy. You can see ornate, polished furniture which has a smell of beeswax and honey.

In a moment you are going to return to the top of the staircase. You are going to count from 20 to one as you descend the stairs gently touching the banister. You are going to give yourself permission to relax and let go both physically and mentally as you become more and more involved with this experience. You may feel a pleasant, relaxed sensation as you focus your entire attention on what your mind is revealing to you. To reinforce this sensation, you allow your breathing to slow down as you reach the hall. Spend a few moments walking around the hall, touching, admiring and marvelling at the intricate craftsmanship and effort which has gone into making the furnishings and wood panelling. You realise you are one of countless people from many generations who have received pleasure from this house and garden. Now you are closer to the grandfather clock, you look to see if there is a date on it, or the maker's name.

At the end of the main hall you notice double doors leading to a dining room with a large table and 10 chairs. The table is laid as if for a dinner party. There is a snowy white tablecloth, silver candelabra, fragrant flowers, crystal glasses and a dinner service. In your mind you can almost imagine the guests and hosts, sitting at the table enjoying the conversation and the taste of the food and the fine wines. Can you picture in your mind what sort of food they are eating? How is the room lit? Is there an open fire? Does it have logs or coal?

Another door leads to a sitting room which is furnished with several plush sofas and comfortable armchairs with damask cushions. There are many pictures on the walls and a huge marble fireplace. The floor length windows overlooking the garden have long velvet drapes. You decide you would like to spend some more time outside.

When you are ready you go out of a wooden door at the back of the house. You grasp the wooden handle and as the door swings open you hear the creaking of the hinges. You are pleasantly surprised by the brightness of the day. As you walk out into the garden, you become aware that you are on a stone terrace with 10 steps leading down. You look up at the sky. Are there fluffy white clouds drifting across the horizon? Can you hear the sounds of the birds in the trees? Are there flowers and shrubs in bloom? Has the grass recently been cut, scenting the air with that special smell we all associate with newly mown grass? Is there a pond, fountain or lake in the grounds? Soak up the feelings of your special garden where you can go at any time you wish. You can do this by asking your mind to recreate this image. As you breathe out slowly, descend the worn stone steps, touching the walls as you do so. Do they feel cool or warm?

SUNDAY

When you reach the bottom, notice whether there is a breeze on your face. Can you feel the warmth of the sun? This is your time. Recognise that you can spend as long as you want in this garden, smelling the flowers and shrubs, enjoying walking on the grass or the paths, listening to the birds, gently touching the leaves and marvelling at the incredible design and colours that nature has provided for you.

When you are ready, allow this image to fade away. Notice how your mind and body feel having switched from your everyday channel of life to a channel of memory or fantasy and how rewarding and satisfying that can be. Choose to let the experience enable you to view your everyday life in a more relaxed and enjoyable way.

Conclusion for Sunday

Today we have asked you to see yourself taking this new programme into the future. We have also suggested that you choose to look at your options for Sunday, such as enjoying your food and developing further ways of using your new relaxation and visualisation skills.

End your Sunday with a smile!

APPENDIX I

The benefits of letting go

Relaxation is a wonderful way of helping you to understand your problems clearly. Sometimes the problem itself can be caused by tension, and relaxation exercises and visualisation can help you to control the tension. As soon as you are able to relax you will feel the benefit. You will have increased your own physical and mental calmness. Practising relaxation you will feel less irritable and anxious, you will feel better every day. If someone has annoyed you, your heart will race, your fists will clench, your head will ache, your spirits will be low. If your body is tense, then so is your mind. If relaxation and energy flow through your body then they will also flow through your mind. You will be able to stop and notice your own reaction. If you are relaxed you can look at the situation you are in and decide whether it is worth using up your batteries by losing your temper or becoming anxious. Once you have created tension, it may take some time for you to unwind. If you are able to stay calm this leaves you with energy in abundance to deal with any problems.

It may be right for you to listen twice a day to a relaxation tape and practise some relaxation in the middle of the day. It may be right for you to listen to a relaxation tape once a day just before you go to sleep. You may need to vary your procedure according to what type of day you are having. Your weekends are more relaxing than weekdays. Keep this book somewhere where you can see it easily or put up notices in different rooms that say something as simple as **do it**, or **I am looking forward to relaxing**, whatever seems right to you. If there is something about your unique self that you would like to alter, relaxation followed by a positive image of yourself with the behaviour that you want is both creative and fulfilling.

Enjoy your journey through life, giving time for relaxation, friends and hobbies, and you will have many things to look back on with pride and a sense of achievement.

Making your own recordings

You may find it relaxing to record your own favourite exercises for easy listening at a time that suits you best. Below are a few hints and suggestions that you may find useful.

Where to record

Bear in mind that noises other than your voice will be picked up when recording. While it may be nice to hear birds singing in the background, aircraft, trains or noisy children will not be quite so welcome. Be selective about the time and place of your recording – you will find you get a much better result if you record in a room with curtains and soft furnishings.

Using a different voice

Some people are very self-conscious of how they sound on tape. If this applies to you, why not ask a friend to record for you – this may be more relaxing.

Take your time

Remember, this tape is to be used for relaxation, so prepare your exercises carefully, and record them slowly. You could always record several different sequences to add variety during your relaxation times.

APPENDIX III

Exercises

5 minutes

10 minutes

15 minutes

20 minutes